Mending the Circle

A Guide for Reviving The Ancient Women's Circle

Rev. Liliana Barzola

ISBN: 9781723815201

Cover designed by Theresa Pridemore
Edited by Drew Vandiver & Jennifer Armbrust

DEDICATION

This book is a group effort, even if you only see me here as your guide. There are too many women to mention by name who have helped me birth this book into being.

This book came through like my children. Quietly gestating until I felt like I was going to puke and die all at the same time. I couldn't imagine how something so big was going to come through me.

Two weeks before my daughter's due date, I felt a whoosh when my water broke. I thought, 'okay, I'm having a baby now.' It was unexpected; faster than I thought it would happen. I rode the waves of fear and denial. When the pain is so great, its hard to believe there will be a reward at the end. Birth feels like a bad slumber party I can't leave. I can't call my mom to come save me. During my daughter's labor, I did actually try to run away. I remember my midwife (bless you Lucina!) shoving me back down in the birthing pool and saying, "You're not getting out of this. You can't run away. You have to go through this."

Thank you to my birth coach, editor and long time friend Drew Vandiver, one of the most majestic clowns and talented writers I have ever met.

Gratitude to all the women who have joined my circles. Who had compassion and patience for me as I tried to find my way through the labyrinth of the circle. Each one of you taught me something. Each one of you are an intricate part of this tapestry.

Terri Gregory, thank you for many years of love and support. For initiating me into your accidental circle.

To my chosen madrina (godmother), Maria Grazia, who graciously took me and my son in when we had no place to go. You saved our lives. I will never forget what you did for us.

Thank you Marissa Mayer, my chosen sister. I can't write the rest because I will cry and not be able to see the words through the tears. You have been my constant, even when you were inconsistent.

To my Mother. It feels like everything good in my entire life is because of you. I know you've been watching over me from your preferred vantage point – the angelic realm. The light in your eyes, your smile, your touch... I miss it all. You were my mom for such a short period of time. I feel some days like maybe you weren't even real. Maybe you were just a vision of goodness. One day, I'll really tell your story to the world.

To my sister, Michelle. No doubt living it up in heaven and watching over the little one you left behind who isn't so little anymore. You coached me through so much. You taught me to not stop at defeat and to begin again.

To my daughter, Gabriella. My heart re-formed the day you were born. You are a magnificent spark of courage and strength. You are my teacher. Thank you for choosing me as your mom. To my son, Uriah, who likes to put marshmallows in his tea.

To my chosen sisters, Theresa Pridemore, Tami Kent, Cynthia Lopez, Josie Coleman, Melinda Laus, Rachel Kofron, "Ruby", Mikelle Leis, Laurie Lemieux, Kim Schmith, Martha Ahern and Lucina Armstrong. Thank you, for continuing to choose me, even when I have nothing left to give back.

To Lora Potter, (Harry Potter's long lost sister), you are an amazing gem of an assistant. Thank you for your unending patience and kind words for me when I fucking up everything.

To my beloved, Bri, my sweet talker, my body guard, my guide... The moment I heard your rich, powerful voice I was interested. You were like a body of water to a landlocked mermaid. When my friends found out I was dating a wilderness guide, business strategist and total badass, they were relieved; finally, I would be able to navigate to locations on time. No one has ever made me as angry as you do. You regularly point out when I limit my asks, fear my success and engage in insecurity. I had been programmed by the patriarchy to be small, compliant and uncertain. You showed up in my life only after I decided not to engage with dysfunction. You are the embodiment of the divine masculine. Being with you is fucking scary, but you are so hot it keeps me magnetized. There are very few people in this world that can be charismatic, hilarious and then calmly preform **CPR** or help someone survive a near decapitation. When someone is being disrespectful you call them out, you deescalate and impose right use of power. Your triple Taurus is the match to my Piscean heart.

TABLE OF CONTENTS

1 WELCOME

Whatever good we are seeking is also seeking us.

Any good we have ever known in our family of humankind, will find us again.

The psyche is a universe unto itself in which nothing good is ever truly lost.

Any lost or missing parts to the Holy, we will dream again.

We will ever dream the Holy anew.

–Clarissa Pinkola Estes

I welcome you into our circle.

Feel free to bring your courage, your pain, your tears and your laughter.

Bring your numbness, your defeat, your disappointment, your trauma.

This book is an invitation into the sisterhood, just as you are.

The Grand Mothers know you and you know them.

They have your back.

2 WHY CIRCLE

Women have gathered together in sacred circles since the beginning of time.

In modern times, we mostly don't.

Most of us have forgotten about the sisterhood. We have been pitted against one another. We have gotten lost in ridiculous cultural games that have exhausted us instead of empowering us.

We have been caught up in shaming each other and ourselves.

We have been caught up in trauma and grief and isolation.

We have forgotten the rituals and medicine of gathering in sacred circles.

I am here to remind you, and myself, about the power of the sisterhood. I would like to take you on a journey to remembering. Take my hand and let's do this.

There is no one "right" way to do a sacred circle. There are as many different ways to gather and have ceremony as there are lineages.

My lineage information has mostly been forgotten. I come from migrators. Almost every generation was traveling to a new place. They were courageous, adventurous and often looking for something more. It's in my blood. My parents came separately from South America to the United States in search of something better. They both came with nothing and they met here. Argentina is a melting pot of ethnicities, just like the United States.

On my grandmother's side, my great-grandfather took a ship from Italy to Argentina and worked for many months, sending back money to his wife and 6 kids. Then one day, he came home to his room at the boarding house and found his wife and six kids had come on their own across the ocean. His wife explained she couldn't live without him anymore. I cannot imagine the courage it took her to immigrate as a single woman with all those kids.

On my grandfather's side in Argentina, my great-grandmother was the neighborhood tea leaf reader. She also read playing cards. Her name was Sarah Murphy and she was the daughter of Irish immigrants.

My dad's side is indigenous to South America and that information has surely been lost. When I met a history teacher from Argentina, I was so excited to get some information about my native lineage. To my chagrin, she scolded me when I asked, "Who are the indigenous tribes of Argentina?" She angrily told me there were no native people in Argentina. It was all Europeans since the beginning of time. Whoa!

So as you can see, I don't have one tradition that has been taught to me. I have a unique fingerprint of a lineage and remembered some of the sacred ceremony and importance of women's circles through my psychic visions and dreaming.

The goal of this book is to help you tap into your own rituals for circle. I hope you use the colors of these stories and exercises on your own canvas. This is a guidebook rather than a rulebook. This information was shared with me in the dreamtime. This Women's Circle exists in the dreamtime. It has always been there. Many of us have forgotten how to tap into it here on Earth.

I share with you my curated version of The Ancient Women's Circle.

3 WHO AM I

I love labels. So I'll start there.

Latina: I consider myself a woman of color. My parents emigrated from South America to the United States in the 60s. I was born on that tipping point where the 70s and 80s dissolve into each other. I grew up with what felt like zero women in the media that looked anything like me. I felt invisible. I loved belly dancing. I know that has nothing to do with South American culture, but when Shakira showed up on the scene, I felt less alone. I am a flawed, mixed-up, confused, cultural masterpiece. My father didn't like us speaking Spanish at home, so my Spanish is really bad. I fought hard in high school to check the box "Hispanic" against the wishes of my family. We were trying to pass as white "Americanos". My mother was light skinned and French-looking with a thick Argentine accent. My father was a dark skinned, dark haired, dark eyed, hand-

14

some beast with a lisp and a thick Argentine accent. I could clearly see we were not passing, de-
spite their efforts. It was obvious because I saw
how my parents were treated. It made me want to
scream.

And sometimes, I did.

I screamed at the woman behind the store counter
who wouldn't help my mother. The woman who tormented my mother (who was speaking clear, under-
standable English) by saying over and over to her,
"Sorry ma'am I just can't understand a word you
are saying." My poor mother was desperately trying
to speak slower and more clearly. Or when I entered
a store with my father and saw the reaction of the
clerk as they kept their eyes on him, making sure he
was there to buy and not steal. And there were
softer, funnier times when I knew I was different.
Like times when I could pick out the single, tex-
tured South American accent in a restaurant full of
loud people. It's almost as if my mother's lullaby

was streaming in under all the audible chaos. Or the time I handed my ID to a bartender and he looked at my name, then at me, and said without a doubt, "You are Argentine." He was like a real life magician to me. He explained that he grew up in Florida and he could track the subtle nuances of Latino culture. My name, my face, it just screamed at him.

Mother: I consider myself a single mother. I have kids from two different partners and although I have been married intermittently, I have been alone in my parenting of them. I struggle to pay the bills for my family like most mamas do. My only inheritance is spiritual and it is worth more than money to me. I spent the majority of my womanhood looking at really put together mommies and longing to be like them. I have recently embraced that I am not them and won't be them. I am terrible at bedtime because I tend to get my kids more riled up with puppet shows and silly accents then calming story time that drifts them to sleep. I sing when I want to scream, and I savor, equally, their sweet laughs and my stolen moments of solitude.

Super-Fem-Lesbian: I just made that one up, as far as I know. I love sparkly shit! I love dressing up. I love shoes and trinkets. I want to help everyone put their make-up on. I am a cis-gendered woman. I have the luxury of having been born into a form that, for the most part, feels right to me. Even with my hormonal surges, aches and pains, I have what I want. I've mostly let go of self-hatred. I have yearned for female lovers but my experiences always led to heartache. Out of grief and fatigue, I spent most of my dating life with male partners. I fit the stereotype of straight feminine woman and it felt like nothing else would fit. I fell in love with a woman who loved me back and then it felt like I could finally have the privilege of the label.

Entrepreneur and Internationally Renowned Psychic: Intuitive since birth. Over the last 18 years, I have built a thriving online and in-person practice. I do psychic readings, energy healing, business consultations and help people develop their own intuition.

Dyslexic: School was unbearably hard for me as a dyslexic child. Putting these words here has been mind numbingly hard. But the pain of keeping them in became too great. If you are dyslexic and reading this, I understand how hard it is for you, I appreciate you showing up and reading this.

Oh yeah, and I **LOVE** to cook.

4 MAMMA'S RAISING A PSYCHIC

My mother would say that my birth healed her. It was the majestic romantic experience she had dreamed of.

But raising me was not.

I was her third child. Her first two births were disempowering experiences. She felt dehumanized by doctors in hospitals and was ahead of her time with the home birth movement. She found herself a midwife, who was Native American, to deliver me at home. During my birth, she reclaimed her power, felt supported and loved. She would say excitedly, "then I stood up from my own bed and took a shower in my own home." As if that was the end all be all. It was adorable when she talked about my birth in this moony way. Then she'd get a really intense look on her face, as if remembering something sour, and it would just be the memory of her sleepless, screaming banshee of a child - me. She said, "You **NEVER** slept. Like, not ever. It was as if you were the spirit that was born to stand watch and couldn't doze. Your nervous system was ready at any moment. And on the off chance you did doze, you woke up angry and upset, as if you had missed something really important."

I was a screamer. She had two mild-mannered daughters before me. I was the one that made her question motherhood. There was a rule in our home to never begin a sentence with the word "no" when speaking to me. I couldn't hear anything afterward that word. She would scold my sisters to "PLEASE say, you CAN have this instead or you CAN do that. Always say the positive thing first, then MAYBE the "no" later." If I heard no, it was like a bomb had gone off in the house. My tiny little body unleashed a torment of shrieks that wouldn't stop.

Slowly, she began to realize that my dramatics came from my sensitivity. She would say that if someone with "bad energy" walked into the room, I would instantly start crying. She always knew when my father was home because I would begin wailing the second his car was in the driveway. My dad came home angry most days. One day, I awoke from a nap calling for my dad. That was strange because I wouldn't even let him hold me normally. This time, I was begging to see him. An hour later, she got a call saying my father was rushed to the hospital because he was having a heart attack. It turned out to just be stress, but it didn't matter. She would tell me that from that moment forward, she knew I had a gift. And she spent the rest of her time trying to help me develop my gifts.

At thirteen years old, she sent me to a "rebirthing meditation" class. I came home so angry with her! "Why didn't you tell me that dad didn't want me?! A little warning would have been nice." She sat in horror as I relayed the entire conversation they had years ago when she told him she was pregnant with me. She apologized and we cried. She had no idea the information would be that clear for me. But it was. It always was.

From the age of 12, I had a ton of babysitting jobs. I could never figure it out because I really wasn't very good with children. I was not a natural at all. Then slowly, over time, the mothers would stop leaving their house when I was watching their children. First, they would linger and, then, they would just stay. I would arrive; they'd sit me down at their kitchen table and offer me tea. We would start chatting. The entire 4 hours would go by and then they would say, "Oh well you were here anyway so here's your pay." Then my mom would pick me back up.

The conversations were usually about their childhood, their husbands, their kids, and their frustrations. I would listen. I would reflect back and I'd offer them some thoughts and advice. Now that I do this for a living. I can look back and see what was happening. These mothers loved the infusion of vibrant feminine energy. I would sit with them and read the situation they were in, offer perspective, encourage them to self-care. I would make these small metaphorical connections and their eyes would glaze over and they'd say, "Wow! That makes so much sense. Yes! That is what is happening. How come I didn't see it before?" Then they'd pay me and off I went.

5 HOLISTIC ACTIVISM

What is Holistic Activism?

The consciousness level of the masses is grotesque-ly low. We have forgotten nature. We have forgotten that there is an entire ecosystem that sustains us humans. In order to go unconscious and deny what we have lost, we zero in on money and materialism. As women, we have been drugged, medicalized, forgotten and renamed a thousand times over.

Still you cannot kill us.

The feminine is life. She is strong, passionate and eternal. In the form of Mother Nature, she's tougher than the patriarchy, bigger than all of us, with her global warming fever, with her tsunami waves and her earth shaking healing. Yes, she cares but as humans have become a virus to her, she remembers to practice self-care first. To remember the Great Mother, we have to mother ourselves first. Do this by nourishing your system with good food, mindfulness and awareness. You are here to help us all remember wholeness and to raise your vibration daily.

This is what I call Holistic Activism.

I see the circle as act of Holistic Activism. Creating a container for our feminine selves to heal and become whole again is just plain rad. In the circles, I have seen prissy, entitled, angry bitches melt their traumatized hearts and get really fucking real. In the circle, you leave behind the bullshit. You can show up putting forth a false version of yourself and, as you reform your shape, you become truly you.

I will give you an example.

Paula was a fist pumping, super positive lady who joined our circle. When it came to sharing, she exuded confidence and excitement about being in our circle. She was **SUPER** positive. However, it was clear that there was pain under there that she wasn't willing to share. Each time she shared, she started by complimenting the other women in our circle. Finally, she would share how wonderful her life was. How perfect everything was. She **NEVER** complained. She was just there to "support the other women."

One by one, each woman came to me asking me to kick her ass out of our circle. She was "not one of us". She was "so fucking chipper" and underneath they felt falseness. They would be in a quiet rage until they had a moment to come to me in private and beg and plead for her membership to be revoked. Now, I never said anything stupid, like, "Now if she's lighting you up, that's just because there is something she is showing you that you don't like about yourself." Because that is one of my most hated pieces of psychological bullshit. Instead, I would validate them and remind them that life happens to everyone. I would say, "of course she's full of utter bullshit, but that isn't her fault".

What I saw was a scared, abused little girl who wanted everyone to like her so they wouldn't kill her. I really, really mean this. Sometimes when we have been traumatized and abused, we learn to blow smoke up everyone's ass to keep them distracted from actually looking at us. A couple months into our circle, little Miss Perfect let me know her entire life was falling apart. She blamed it all on me and my circle. Once again, I validated that was probably true. If there's something to be healed, it will surface. The next time we had group, she broke down. She blamed all the women in the group for her demise and she totally fell apart. Nobody held her crying body, no one tried to save her or make it better. Instead, we held space. We sang and we toned for her. She became one of the most beloved women in our circle after that. She finally felt safe enough to stop lying to herself and she blossomed into wholeness.

This is Holistic Activism.

It might not be a Keto diet and wearing yoga pants, but it's being real about the state we are truly in.

6 THE SISTERHOOD

After my sister Michelle died, I was struggling to make sense of her life and death. She was an amazing woman, a hero of mine. She was my big sister. Michelle was diagnosed with cancer at 27 and died the year my son was born. She was 31 years old. Her death was exceptionally hard because her final wishes were not honored by the religion that she had been a part of. In her transition my mother and I were unable to advocate for her. It was the most excruciating thing I have ever had to witness. To stand by and watch my sister be tormented by the very people that she trusted was unbearable. It is hard for me to even write this now.

My mother and I held each other close through it all. And although my loss was great, seeing my mother go through the loss of a child seemed far worse. Shortly after Michelle's passing, my mother and I went to a spiritual lecture. Not much of the lecture was reaching us in our grief-hazed state. However, there was one particular line that made its way into our minds and hearts. That line was, "If you are grateful you cannot suffer."

It showed us that much of our processing around Michelle's death was on the betrayal and sadness. There was no room left for celebrating my sister. From that moment on, we used that one line to help each other focus on the magic my sister brought to us. It helped us feel her presence.

My mother, in some ways, was more like a sister to me. She was really good at making us all feel important. Each one of us would say that we were my mother's favorite. Even still, my childhood wasn't especially supportive. There was a tension between my two sisters that was damaging to me as a child. My mother also had trouble standing up for herself in her marriage. However, over the years, we all began to get healthier. I even saw my sister's passing as an act of health. It was the only way she knew to get out of an abusive relationship with her ex.

The concept of sisterhood wasn't fully formed for me until my mother and I had two versions of the same dream.

One morning, my mother called to tell me about a dream she'd had about my sister. I also wanted to share a dream. In her dream, she was talking on the telephone to someone and then all of a sudden the line cut out and a woman's voice she instantly recognized as my sister Michelle spoke. She said, "I am calling from the sisterhood." My mom was obviously overjoyed to hear my sister's voice. She wondered, in the dream, if maybe my sister hadn't died after all. My sister playfully said, "Don't worry, mom. I am with the sisters; I am calling you from the sisterhood. We will all be ok."

In my dream, I came home to find my sister in my living room. She was lying in a hospital bed and telling me that she was, in fact, alive. She managed to escape from Stanford hospital. She said, "I am with the sisterhood now. I am not dead, I am alive."

Different dreams with the same message and same

phrase. There is life after death and that is what my sister was reminding us of. She cannot be gone. That is clear. Just like the Ancestors and the Grandmothers and the women who have inspired you. They are all here with us now. All you need to do is ask. Ask for guidance. Ask for support. Ask for love. The sisterhood is alive and well. We are all part of this sisterhood. You are not alone.

What is sisterhood? Those of us who have sisters and love them, feel safe and bonded, probably have a lot of positive things to say on this subject. Those of us who hate our sisters have a different story to tell. Sisterhood is, for me, a chosen alliance. It's the women who I can turn to in moments of weakness and they don't judge me. They don't problem solve and try to fix me. They simply witness me and hold space for me to figure my shit out.

My sister Michelle was this for me. Even when I drove her crazy, she was still my ally. At the same time, my relationship with my other sister was not so golden. We are very different people. The only thing we have in common is shared trauma. I love her, but I don't understand her and she has no idea who I am. And that's okay. We don't need to do some forced bonding ritual.

I invite you to create your own sisterhood. And also to know that you don't need to love all the women in circle. You might really hate some of them. Because they remind you of something that doesn't feel right. They might not be your cup of tea and that's okay. The sisterhood respects and supports diversity. It is vital that we don't interfere with peoples' growth processes.

What the world needs now most of all is women who are willing to tell their stories and to listen to the stories of other women. To accept that we have very common experiences and very different ones. We don't all have to agree on everything in order to mend the circle and ourselves. The circle is a safe container for the sisterhood to replenish. You actually don't need all these rituals and work-sheets. You might throw them all out when the dance goes longer than expected or the meal you are enjoying is too good to cut short for a work-sheet. The circle is not rigid. The circle is fluid.

In my childhood, I felt more oppressed than uplifted by women. School girls weren't to be trusted. I had this innocence and natural love for women that usually left me feeling shamed, burned, betrayed. I gradually walled up my heart until much later in life, when I had adult female friends who showed me what sisterhood could feel like. When I was pregnant with my first child, I desperately wanted to host a dinner at my home. But I didn't have a kitchen table. One of my friends loaded her own kitchen table into her truck and drove it to my home so I could have the experience I so desired. Little moments like these over the years have helped me overcome my trust issues.

I was born with a desire to empower and advocate for women. I have seen the power that women hold. And when we are healthy and empowered, we can move mountains. The number one ally women have is each other. The patriarchy has divided us. I happen to think all the world's problems will be solved when there is equality "for us all" regarding genders. That feels like the special recipe to me.

7 THE GRANDMOTHERS

What the GrandMothers want you to know:

They are protecting all of us.

They have elegance, grace, power and patience.

They keep us safe.

They also protect information from being lost or misused.

You are safe and secure because the GrandMothers are holding you at all times. They have been present since the moment of your creation and are available to give you guidance and messages if you ask.

There is a circle of women that reside in the astral realm.

They are the GrandMothers. They offer comfort, welcome and nurture us.

The Grand Mothers are calm and hopeful because they understand that healing is occurring.

They are not afraid.

They are active and available at all times.

They hold the best interest of us all within their hearts.

The feminine essence (Yin) is growing and healing our earth. It is creating the balance that is needed.

They are whole and they help us all to be whole.

In the west, we have lost our understanding of the Grand Mothers. Grand Mothers initiate us into the spiritual world by reminding us of our traditions. A tradition is an understanding of nature put into practice. Think of seasons and farming. Many traditions are just best practices for nature. It's important that we question traditions and update them. If we don't, we just become programmed. Operating with blind faith is never a good practice.

A Grand Mother embodied is not an old woman,

necessarily, but a wise one. She just casually drops her wisdom and asks for nothing in return.

The Grand Mothers will find you, support you and come to your aid. Imagine you are moving out on your own for the first time. At a thrift store, you are sorting through pots and pans, trying to figure out what you might need. Suddenly, a mature woman casually swoops in and tells you exactly the answer to the question in your head. She drops wisdom and disappears.

Soon after my mother's passing, I had two mind-blowing visits from Grand Mothers.

In the first visit, I was catching an 8-hour flight with a wiggly toddler. I was taking my mothers ashes to Hawaii so she could swim with the tortugas/honu. I felt non-functional in my grief. I had a hell of a time getting through security with her ashes and was overwhelmed with my toddler. We were sitting in a center aisle when a man tapped my shoulder. "Pardon me, ma'am, my wife is happy to help you with your baby." He had kind eyes and a really grounded feel to him. Yet, in my haze, I couldn't understand a word of his statement. Before I could answer, my toddler reached for him across the aisle and crawled across his lap to his wife seated by the window. She smiled and mouthed, "it's okay, I'm here to help." It made me want to burst into tears. A couple hours later, I awoke from a slumber, horrified that my child was still with strangers. How could I be so irresponsible, giving my child to someone on a freaking plane! I looked over to see him happily playing. For four hours, this Grand Mother talked to him, pointed to stuff, he played with her hands, almost in a trance. The best part (all the mamas will get this), when she handed him back, he fell asleep on me the entire rest of the flight. Usually when people take your kid to help you, your kid falls instantly to sleep, only to be woken when you return and they are filled with rocket fuel. Not this time. Instead, I got to cuddle a sleeping baby and enjoy him for the rest of my heartbreaking flight.

The second visit from a Grand Mother was when my son was 4 years old. He was angry and refused to go into the grocery store with me. It was the last stop before we got to go home after a really long day. I was fed up and exhausted and he defied all reason. No amount of me explaining this was a "quick stop" for food he desperately needed, we had "nothing at home", I could get him a snack to eat immediately... nope, nothing worked. Finally, I dragged him out of the car, kicking and screaming, but lost my fuel when we hit the sidewalk of the grocery store. I said, "Okay, you stay out here." I walked into the grocery store without him, leaving him to sit dangerously on the curbside. To my horror, he didn't follow. I watched, hidden, from the window. Then along came a Grand Mother. She sat down next to him. Thoughts ran through my mind that the police would be called for the abandoned child. I watched him get to his feet. He took her hand and walked into the store. She walked right up to me with a soft smile, a giggle in her eyes and said, "I think he's ready now."

When Grand Mothers visit, they are generous.

The moment is profound.

You will definitely know.

You will be powerless to stop them from helping and their help will, in the end, actually feel like help.

8 MY FIRST CIRCLE

I experienced my first "women's circle" quite by accident.

In 2008, a client, Terri, invited me to celebrate the soft opening of her new Bed and Breakfast in Monmouth, Oregon. Terri invited five of the women who helped her launch her new business for a complimentary night at the B and B. As excited as I was to join in, I felt nervous. I didn't know what to expect or any of the women who were participating. I thought about canceling, even on the drive in.

I was immediately awestruck by her bright blue Victorian with New Orleans flavor and decor. The house was designed and named in memory of Terri's grandmother, her MaMere. As a child, Terri had been told negative stories about her wild and reckless grandmother. When Terri was going through a divorce, she began wondering if those stories about her grandmother were really true. Maybe her grandmother was just a self-made, liberated woman in a time of serious feminine oppression. She chose to celebrate that version of her MaMere instead. Terri entertained us with stories of MaMere lodging strangers for money and making moonshine in the bathtub, all to keep her many children fed. I fell instantly in love with the idea of this wild woman.

MaMere's felt like an exotic getaway in a small town with a little French pioneer history. The house colors are intense and vibrant, without overpowering you. As you enter the foyer, you step back in time and geography. It has an Old World feel to it.

I entered the kitchen to meet the vibrant and delightful chef, Kary. This woman was a culinary master. She made everything from scratch. I sat in the cherry red kitchen with tin ceiling tiles, watching her grate fresh lemon for the homemade lemon bars. I found myself laughing and chatting with her and another woman, Jody. Jody was striking with her deep red hair and white terrycloth robe, a generous smile and glistening eyes. She said that when Terri told her she was inviting some amazing women over for the weekend, she begged to be included. Something told me she didn't exactly beg for the invitation. She was a great addition. Jody was next in line for a massage. This was one of Terri's luxurious surprises. We were each receiving a treatment in the massage room. Terri's friend Summer was getting a treatment from the masseuse, Elizabeth.

I got a detailed tour, while Terri offered my choice of the available rooms. Each room was like a character in a movie, with either a supporting or starring role. The luxurious guest rooms had names like, Starry Night, Le Marti Gras Muse, The Magnolia Room, and French Toast. I chose The Magnolia Room. It was rich and delicious, like raspberry sorbet. There was a large bed with abundant drapery and a painted magnolia on the ceiling that envelops you as you lay on the soft bed. You feel like a honeybee, wrapped up into a flower, laying on the plush bed, looking up.

The backyard had a wonderful gazebo with lights that spiraled up in the center. The whimsical backyard washes away exhaustion and the to-do list. We sat relaxing under the gazebo, chatting and enjoying the perfect summer weather, as the kitchen's tantalizing scents drifted into the yard.

Tami arrived with her angel of a child, Japhie, 14 months old, blond with blue eyes. She looked like a mama kangaroo, wearing her baby. Cheese and wine appeared and the goat cheese was out of this world. These were some happy goats.

After Jody's massage, Tami went into the massage room for her treatment, while Terri and I took Japhie for a stroll. When we returned, Tami was sitting in her massage afterglow and curled into a comfortable chair to nurse her gorgeous child.

Dinner was served. New Orleans-style Jambalaya, an elegant salad, and warm bread rolls slathered with butter. Through glasses of red wine, we giggled and teared up, laughed robustly and sat silently. All the colors of the rainbow. The conversation was as nourishing as the food.

As the clock strikes 9pm, from the shadows emerges a miniature black poodle puppy by the name of James Brown. His human mother trails behind. Louisa was an enigmatic healer, a Latina medical doctor turned acupuncturist and activist for Autistic Children. She moves effortlessly into our circle and settles deep into a glass of port wine. Her eyes glisten in the twinkling lights as she shares the stories of her amazing work with autistic children. On this night, I am surrounded by a medical doctor turned acupuncturist and child advocate, authors, healers, grief counselors, and a physical therapist who heals women with her holistic pelvic care, creatrixes all. On that night, I was in the midst of powerful and loving women. If felt like medicine for my soul.

I tapped into a longing I hadn't recognized until it was being fed to me. I recalled being a small child, in the kitchen with my mother, my aunt and big sisters encircling me, conversing and braiding each other's hair, eating and laughing. I remembered feeling safe and loved by women. As an adult woman, these opportunities to "red tent" don't present themselves anymore. Sitting under the twinkling gazebo lights with lush, laughing ladies, I tried to pause time.

I often forget to take time for myself. Time away from being a mom and business owner, away from housework and meetings. I loved the flow of being served like a queen and simultaneously taking turns, helping with baby, getting tea, making plates of food for one another.

I forgot how much I enjoy watching women of all ages and temperatures enjoying themselves. Wearing white spa robes and not worrying about pulling them tight, round curves and breasts is something to be celebrated. It was liberatingly immodest!

As Chef Kary dined with us, she told us the story of her mother's cooking. How she had been the only farmer's wife who cooked with spices in her small town and how this made the food come alive. Kary immersed herself in the smells of her mother's kitchen as she intuited the recipes and flavorful touches.

We shared stories of grandmothers and mothers expected to carry the load of responsibilities alone and through dark times. Women who were considered bad because they felt lost in it. We shared thoughts and hopes that we were transcending many of those ancestral agreements and paving our own roads.

Sitting there under the stars late into the night, I felt heard and understood. Like I didn't have to pave my road alone. An epiphany hit me! Wow! I can be independent and have support!

Homemade dessert, tea, and coffee. As the night turned chilly, we slipped up to our rooms and into warm beds. I slept soundly and peacefully. I felt loved.

In the morning, I tried to sleep in, but was too ex-cited to see my ladies again. I slipped into my soft spa robe and headed down into the sitting room, across from an exquisite drawing of Terri's Grand-mother, MaMere. You can see a glimpse of Terri in her.

I settled in on a beautiful couch, reading a book, greeted by the early rising chef. As Kary buzzed in the kitchen, the scents of fresh coffee and muffins seep into the sitting room. Soon Louisa entered the room with her playful poodle. We sat and talked about the enneagram book she's brought to share. I listened intently, trying to unravel the mystery of the number 8 that she thinks I might be.

Soon Terri and Jody flow in, then Baby Japhie and Tami. It's delicious seeing these women laze around in their PJ's.

Breakfast is a feast of grilled peaches with cinnamon, cardamom, and brown sugar delight, warm oatmeal, fresh fruit and a liquored cream put atop the peaches. Baby moves from lap to lap, exploring the unbaby-proofed living room, which makes for entertainment. Puppy and baby comically share their raisins.

Tami suggests a blessing circle in which we all hold hands and say a blessing for Terri's new venture. We giggle and make sounds, we howl and we listen intently to the next blessing. Nine times around the circle. Terri tells us the story of a woman who out did the men with her accordion playing. On that note, Terri debuts the singer, whose deep soulful voice takes us in to the zydeco music. We all break into spontaneous dance. The music gets intense, our bodies warmed up, robes came off, and baby dances. The circle swells until someone glides into the center to show off their moves. With delightful squeals and hearty whoops, we cheered each other on.

Heated and sweaty, we step out into the yard, into the cool morning air. We said our goodbyes before heading upstairs to pack. All vowing to come back, and so I shall...

9 TOXIC FEMININE

Women's groups and circles can become sick and sad places. The unhealthy feminine prototype is like those women trapped in animal form from my dream (more on that soon). They need more tending and mending before they can step up to lead a group. And that's okay. It's better to say, "I don't want to lead" than to forge on. There's no longevity in lying.

Many of us have stories to tell of looking to our feminine counterparts for protection and support and instead we were humiliated and abandoned, as a result we can become hyper-vigilant. It's exhausting really.

Currently, I identify as a lesbian. I have a front row seat to homophobia. I see all externalized homophobia as internalized homophobia. When someone is homophobic I immediately know they are gay. I see the self-hatred a mile away. Homophobic people work hard to take the shame they feel and put it upon someone else.

When women cut each other down I see this as internalized misogyny. It's the judgmental comparisons and insecurities that we spew onto others instead of dealing with our own shit. The worst type of darkness for me is seeing women in toxic competition with each other. Don't we want our daughters to surpass us in talents, brains, skills and beauty?

When I was nineteen years old, my New Age-loving mama signed us up for a class. We were going to learn to be "psychics" in this one-day workshop. She was really pumped. About 15 minutes into class it was clear to me the teacher lacked personal skills, humility or kindness.

She was teaching everyone to channel and float away from their bodies; for me this is always a recipe for disaster. Escapism packaged as spirituality is dangerous as fuck! It's not a shortcut to enlightenment. The New Age movement is always going to be filled with shiny caricatures of "LOVE" and "ONENESS".

Translation: There are a shit ton of fucked up people dispensing spiritual advice. We need to be discerning.

I was highly entertained by this poor little witch in front of me. She was insecure and ungrounded. About an hour in my mother started feeling light-headed and nauseated. Every exercise this woman had us doing was moving us further away from our bodies. It was like doing somersaults after a milk-shake. My mother's sickness was a sign of her health. I refused to do a single thing she instructed because it was just plain unhealthy. Instead I was meditating and observing. The circle of women were gushing and idolizing her.

I was respectful but didn't allow myself to get manipulated by her.

My mother grew up in a generation with less autonomy, less permission and more oppression. She told me a childhood story of having a beloved art teacher. One day he offered a special group of students a chance to come over to his house and watch a movie about art. This was a big honor.

When she got there he played a pornographic film of bestiality. She was horrified. She was paralyzed with fear. She went home lied to her parents about what had happened and was sick for the next three days. Lots of women have stories like this to tell. They engage in an innocent activity only to be groped or raped by someone. It is the end of innocence and the beginning of understanding how fucking terrible women are treated all over the world.

During our psychic class, my mother began to bravely express her sickness to the instructor. The woman basically just started to take her further out of her body. My mother felt worse. The teacher finally offered the idea that my mother was spiritually inferior. She went around and asked the other students out loud if they were "feeling sick" and since they were fine my mother was clearly the problem. This is classic spiritual manipulation! A grounded, healthy person in a group gets attacked for speaking up about something the group is in agreement to be in denial about.

Finally, I interrupted the abuse. I calmly said, "Okay mom we are leaving now." The woman literally put her body between my mother and I as if I was the culprit. I just laughed at her. What transpired next was an extraction. As the woman began to yell at me for interrupting the abuse, I spoke to a woman in the circle I knew. I said, "Hey I need your help carrying my mother out of here." I broke the spell for a moment. The woman assisted me, taking one arm and I took the other. I got my mother into the backseat of her car. The entire time, the woman was infuriated. I had to shove her out of the car and shut the door. I remember writing her a check from my mother's checkbook. I was like here's your money now please let us be.

As I began to drive us away, my mother's sickness began to lift. We went home and processed what had happened. My mother was totally stuck in the trauma from her childhood. The idea of living through another experience like that was daunting, so her body threw a much needed tantrum to get out of it. No matter how much she wanted to comply she couldn't without puking her guts out.

Sadly, the instructor missed an opportunity for healing!

When someone is struggling in group, we can always adjust. The last thing we want to do is personalize their experience and narcissistically make it about us. She could have supported my mother fully in using her voice, empowered her, helped her practice leaving and coming back, or just let her go with a positive vibe.

Instead I had to carry her out physically. When my mother and I debriefed she got a good laugh and on her own connected it back to that childhood trauma. And as she so often did, she saw and validated my bright new feminine energy. She admired it in me.

I know I only have the privilege of using my voice and tools because she so clearly fought for me even when she couldn't fight for herself.

I have had women leave my circle and it is okay. It doesn't mean you've done anything wrong. Check in with them. Honor them for speaking up. Honor them for self-advocating. Honor them for not belonging.

It's all okay. Maybe the thing they needed to experience for healing most is being able to leave.

10 VIOLENCE AGAINST WOMEN (TOXIC MASCULINE)

You might be wondering what a chapter like this is doing in this book.

I'm not going to put statistics here on how many women are effected by violence. I don't need to.

My first experiences with aggression started with my father. He was a fun loving, gregarious man at work and an angry, stressed-out drunk at home. I remember constantly walking on tiptoes around him, never knowing when he was going to rage.

The unhealthy masculine prototype doesn't want to feel emotions. They need to wall up in order to operate in the world. They don't want to come home to a household of emotions. Men who are not living in their truth and authenticity come home to hate themselves and their lives. As they sit, working to oppress their anxiety and panic, they want silence.

They want to be "respected", to be treated like a king for all the hard work they've done out in the world. All I knew as a child was that my dad was never there and when he was he wanted absolute silence. My mother worked anxiously to keep us quiet. Usually during our family ritual of dinnertime, things were the most intense. My father wanted a nice quiet family meal of no talking. We laughed and played with our food. Also, I was a big choker. My father would go into an absolute rage at the dinner table when I was choking on my food. Think about it from my perspective: I am totally terrified, can't breath and my mom is whacking me on my back while my father rages at us.

From his perspective, he couldn't deal with anything more after the stress of his workday. He couldn't handle a ripple in the pond. Coming home to four kids was full of ripples. My near-death dinner experiences were too much for him to handle. At some point during dinner he would pound his dark giant fist on the table and rage.

"NO LAUGHING!"

"NO TALKING"

Things that just seemed absurd even to my little kid self.

I thought this was normal. My mom taught me to feel compassion for my dad over my own emotional pain. She would tell us about his difficult childhood, how much he worked to support us, how hard it was to be an immigrant in this new American life.

So I learned that men were aggressive ragers and we all needed to enable them by letting them be themselves. While we hid in the corners, hoping they would feel serene again.

I had no other prototype. I didn't know there was any other kind of non-scary masculine.

I remember my mother crying to our male neighbor one day. At first, she was casually sharing how difficult it was getting her kids to bed and how upset it made my dad. She was asking him for tips and ideas because she had such a hard time keeping everyone happy.

Our neighbor was sort of dumbfounded as to what she was asking him. He said, "Elena, what do you mean? That is so normal. They are children. Kids ask for water, then go back to bed, then they need a snack." He was laughing as he said this. The ease in his tone and levity about parenthood was shocking to her. She immediately started crying. She fell totally apart feeling the energy of a man who had a bandwidth for his wife and his children. It was just enough for her to know that this type of healthy masculine energy existed. She got therapy and empowered herself.

I went out into the world, encountering some healthy partners. I danced around the dating world, not being afraid of men anymore. And then I married an ax murderer. Ha, ha. Nope. I married an abusive, unstable, bipolar, alcoholic and had a child with him. I have experienced domestic violence and it fucking sucks.

I didn't realize I was in an abusive relationship until I watched an episode of Oprah. (Yup, you just read that right.) In 2005, I was watching Oprah interview "everyday women" who are were being abused. They were strong women like me. They didn't take shit from their partners. However because of their strength, over time, those women gave up more and more of their sanity in an effort to stabilize their unstable partners.

Abuse doesn't show up on our Instagram feeds as pictures of physical or emotional wounds one partner has inflicted on another. Because abuse has a cycle, the abused partner may post happy pictures, hand holding, love bombing when things are good. This furthers the illusion, wanting to show themselves and the world that it's not that bad.

This is my message for every person who is being abused in their relationship right now: It's not your fault. You are over-functioning and you don't have to continue. Your heart will feel lighter once you leave.

Maybe you don't recognize you are being abused. Maybe you don't know what freedom feels like. I didn't.

Are you in denial about the unhealthy toxic relationship you exist in? I have been in denial more than once and more than twice...

Do you?

-Tiptoe around your partner's moods

-Feel like you have to parent them

-Feel unsafe emotionally or physically

-Feel controlled and undermined by your partner

Do they?

-Say abusive things

-Give you dirty or threatening looks

-Rage or tantrum

-Act aggressively

-Shame and humiliate you

Maybe you are afraid to leave because of investment bias. You are so invested up to this point, it feels harder to leave than to stay.

Fears:

-If you leave maybe you won't ever have a baby?

-If you leave how will it be for your kids when you've been the one holding everything together?

-If you leave will you lose your lifestyle?

I left an abusive relationship when I had a 3-year-old child and no place to go. So if I can do it, you can do it.

Here's my story. I was married with a beautiful little baby. My husband started off as a wonderful partner. He was patient with our child and with me. He changed diapers, did loads of house work, cooking and parenting. We had opposite work schedules so our little boy was always with one or the other. It seemed pretty perfect. He was easy going, fun and loving and we had a good life together.

He had been married before me to the "love of his life". Once in a while, he would have too much to drink and spend the night lamenting and crying about his previous wife. It was really heartbreaking to watch, but being a loving wife, I would listen and support him. I never felt jealousy, just a deep well of compassion for his pain and process.

One night, our son was very sick and so was I. I

couldn't get a hold of him after work and was wondering why he wasn't coming home. He had turned his phone off and was getting drunk at the bar. We had a long talk when he returned. Over time, slowly these episodes happened more frequently.

-He was driving home intoxicated in our brand new car.

-He was drinking and smoking his paycheck away.

-He would become so angry and belligerent, I would have leave the house when he was shouting and threatening me. I would go out into the street and just wait for him to calm down with our baby in my arms.

-I didn't tell anyone this was happening because it was so shocking and after each time it felt like we got to a new place of understanding and behavior would change for a while.

-I was embarrassed this was happening to me.

-I felt unsafe during his tirades, however, I never thought he would ever physically harm me. I was watching someone who was having a trauma response. I worked with him to get our family through it. (This is called denial, over-functioning and code-pendence.)

Suddenly, my mother passed away and I had no bandwidth for his drama anymore. I could no longer deny that he had a full blown drinking problem. I asked him to get help but it became clear there were some big mental health issues I could not help him with.

I asked him for a separation and to try dating each other once some space was given. I didn't want to lose my family. The night before our first couple's therapy session I came home to count 14 empty beer bottles on the counter and my husband passed out next to our 3-year-old son. He woke up and began shouting at me. Then he tried to strangle me. And all the while, he was calling me by his ex wife's name. I remember the moment he looked into my eyes as my airway was being cut off. I went limp and just decided to let him kill me. That was the moment he stopped. But then he began again. And then he stopped again. I grabbed the phone. I called the police. He wouldn't let me take the baby and just leave and I was not leaving my baby with him!

He immediately began dumping drugs down the toilet and then came back into the living room and calmly started folding laundry. The 911 operator asked me what he was doing. I couldn't bring myself to say "folding laundry". Because that seemed absurd considering what he had actually done to me. I slowly began to understand that this was his game. Years later, when he tried to drag me out of my car during a pick-up, I had my newborn daughter and my 9-year-old son in the car. He was so calm as he was hurting me, he kept saying calmly to me, "you are doing this to yourself. You are the one that is doing this."

I remembered in my panic, not being able to stay in the car, he was too strong. He was overpowering me as he was calmly talking to me. In my struggle to break free of him I was screaming and I was slamming the door on his enormous arms and he would not let me go. I remember thinking why is he not getting hurt by this door? And why am I trying to hurt him in front of my son? And my poor daughter is hearing me scream. I am out of control. He is right. It is so hard to unravel the victim mind. It's so hard to fight in these moments. I started driving the car down the street with him half in and half out. And I was afraid I was going to kill him. Even though he was trying to kill me.

He was still there. He was still overpowering me. With my right hand, I grabbed my phone and started calling 911. He then let me go and I drove off. I hung up on the police. Because I was afraid I would be the one in trouble.

I didn't want his son to have to see the cops take us away.

I pulled over the car down the street because I couldn't drive safely until I calmed myself. That is when I heard my son ask me, "Mom, why didn't you stay on the call and have him arrested?"

I realized what an idiot I was, again. The first night the police came, I lied and told them he didn't touch me. I remember the cops absolutely knew I was lying to them. I didn't want him to go to jail or lose his job. I just wanted to be able to take my baby to safety.

I used to think that victims of domestic violence were weak and wondered why they would stay. I share these experiences with you now because I consider myself a strong woman who has been a survivor of domestic violence. I was strong then and I am strong now. I didn't relate to the idea of a victim mentality. A victim is a weak person who can't fend for themselves. What I've unearthed is that my victim mentality was me thinking I could fix my partner. It was me excusing his behavior and only holding myself accountable. So I needed a new phrase. Instead of "victim mentality", I like thinking I was an "out-of-control healer". It's me thinking I could stabilize someone else. It was me in denial that my partner was changing form. It's a wishful thinking that is detrimental to my health, my life, my survival. It's my family of origins dysfunction coming back to haunt me.

If you are in a situation that is abusive, I under-stand where you are. I encourage you to speak up to someone who feels safe and who will support you in a way and at a pace that feels good to you. If you know someone in an abusive relationship, don't rush them to leave. Invite them to be healthy. Encourage them to figure out what is right for them. They will find their way home.

11 THE IMPORTANCE OF REST

Historically women's accomplishments have been ignored, dumbed down and covered up.

The things women create and accomplish are mind-blowing! From enduring the most intense pain imaginable (birthing babies) to managing all the tangible regulatory things in life, all the while taking care of others. We take care of people, children, animals, villages, etc. We do this with our very presence. No one can truly see or comprehend all that you do.

That is why it is vital that you practice self-compassion, love and that you **REST**.

That you stand up for yourself.

That you rest even when others think you should work harder.

No one can truly know the effort that you put forth in your everyday life. The expectations are grand and never ending. The accolades are slim.

You may have experienced traumatic moments. The force of it creates an invisible shattering into a million pieces. When dealing with the shock and trauma, we still have to function in the world. Doesn't that totally suck? Many of us are working full time, taking care of pets, managing a household, taking care of children, making sure everyone is loved, touched, fed and talked to. We are working to pay the bills and be good to our friends. What if someone announces that you are not doing enough? How does that affect you?

Forgive yourself for all the shit that will be left undone. Even when we give it our all, there will still be laundry to fold. Accepting that you have done your best is key to surviving in this world.

Others will be ignorant about what you do or how hard you work. When people are invalidating and critical toward me, it's often about their own un-reasonable expectation for themselves. In these moments I HAVE to take care of myself. I HAVE to hold myself, rock myself, nurse myself. Celebrate all that I am because I will never be enough for this world.

I can only be enough for me.

And my house may not be clean.

12 THE DREAM

When I laid my 4-month-old baby down, I had this amazing dream that changed the course of my life forever!

My daughter, seven years old now, likes to say, "Mom, it was really more of a vision than a dream."

The ritual and ceremony of this circle helps all of our sisters. On whatever planet, place, time or form they are in. In this circle, women read the energetic messages that the feminine is sending out, story-telling it, recording it, remembering it and holding space for all feminine essence. This is a repairing process. The women of this circle are all purpose-fully focused on healing the feminine essence.

I didn't live past girlhood in my last lifetime on earth, when this circle was active. I did not live as a woman in this particular circle, I was a child. It was clear that the women in the circle were sharing this information with me because I hadn't experienced it as a woman. They were initiating me as a woman and Gabriella, my daughter, as girl/maiden.

A group of women were talking and sharing this information so that I can remember this Ancient Women's Circle. I am realizing that I was once a part of it. It is very emotional for me. My mother, Elena, was a high priestess in this circle. She was the Artist archetype. (I will explain later) My mother helped make the figurines we used in ceremonies. These are small to large figurines made from clay/ceramic.

Here are the women that I recognize: my aunt Lucy, my sisters Michelle and Paula, Marissa, Terri, some of the women from my church from when I was a child and some other women I did know but just can not remember.

(You may have been part of this circle, too. Not sure. You will know if this information is familiar. If not, you have a different circle you belong to. I also feel that women move all around the circles, so maybe at one time you were a part of this circle. This one I know is part of my particular lineage.)

I am sure all women had a circle with their own traditions.

Here are the traditions I was reminded of in the dream.

We are in an old house that seems like MaMere's B and B because it holds the energy of the feminine principles.

There are elder women and younger women. And that is important because the elders work together with the little ones to become a part of the circle.

The purpose of the circle:

To Gather Information (by reading energy and re-membering).

To Protect the Animals.

To Balance the things that are out of balance in the universe; through sight and telling stories.

To Share and Support Each Other.

Here is how the women share this information with me: They talk exactly like women do in a group. Quickly sharing a piece of information and then someone else adds to it. The flow is feminine. What some women remembered, others didn't. So each woman brings an additional piece of the remembering. When a woman spoke, you knew it was a truth and we were all remembering together.

Rules of the circle:

No one is ever made to feel afraid.

Everyone is sacred.

Everyone is here because they are important.

Everyone wants to be here.

The concept of "obligation" is irrelevant. Everyone has a purpose. Like a symphony, each woman has her own unique purpose. Competition doesn't exist. It is not even a concept.

The circle is not a completely round circle. Some women are missing and some women haven't arrived yet.

This circle was recreated on the earth many times but its blueprint is in the astral and will always be there. These circles get created anytime we send the feminine essence somewhere else or into a particular form to gather information or do healing/teaching there. The circle is like a headquarters for healing. It looked like a grid or a network that was reconnecting lost parts of feminine essence back to the whole.

The Grand Mothers tend to sit on the outer part of the circle and the younger women toward the inner or center. So it almost looks more like points on a star. The circle is a star.

The Barn: The barn surrounds the meeting place. We are in the center of it. Animals live here. We are caring for them. I only saw ones that looked like horses. It was clear that some of the women from our circle were trapped in the animal form. We, as a group, had to protect them. Some of the horses and animals were sick. Mostly mentally sick.

Grand Mothers facilitate the energy reading and ceremonies. They also remind us of the guidelines. When reminding, this is never done as a control tactic. It is only when a women is struggling that they are reminded of the Way. The Grand Mothers offer the reminding and it is clear that they are just showing a Way. Some things are absolute and those are truths but the Way is the way things have been done. It is all focused on assisting and supporting. As they were prepping me to bring Gabriella into the circle, I felt it was a great honor to be part of the circle. Since I was never in it as an elder or woman, they were teaching me how to do it all.

Archetypes: Some women are the Grand Mothers (protectors of all of us and the information), some are the Artists (they make the tools for ceremony and much more), some are Seers (the storytellers and readers), some are Healers (laying on of hands and touching things to bring them back to life), some are called the Gardeners (Guardians of the animals and the plants). These women are taking direct care of real animals in the barn, they rotate in and out of the circle.

I can tell you what your archetype is if you want me to.

Ceremony: No one is made to feel afraid; nothing about the ceremony is scary. It is something powerful that brings strength and peace. The power is respected.

There is an understanding that all women, and especially the ones of the circle, must work together as a team, remembering and supporting.

There are no power or control issues because none of the women are analyzing or using their minds.

We are all in our feeling and intuition and this is a level of mastery that must be reached on earth, in the astral, on other planets and all over the place. Meditation is not a new concept and not one particular to the earth. All beings must learn to balance the mind because it is overwhelming, no matter where you are or what form you are in. It is true that the imbalance of the mind is far more aggressive on Earth.

The universe does send out caricatures of these concepts to remind us. Like Gurus. Gurus viewed as carnival people from the dreamtime. They are flashy to remind the people on earth about these concepts.

Harmonizing: When talking, they each take their turn, like an amicable flow of support and sharing information. No one is fighting or contradicting each other. If this were to happen, they would all do something called Harmonizing. For example, they tone like: La la la la la. They do this for a moment, one woman starts when she senses stress in the space or if there are dark energies surrounding or affecting the circle. When this happens, everyone starts harmonizing. And then just keeps on point. This never happened when I was there. But they explained and demonstrated. It was clear it wasn't needed too often. But it wasn't questioned when someone started Harmonizing. We all followed in support and agreement for safe space. It could even be that individual woman's fear. It didn't matter. If she started, we all joined in. And the conversation picked back up immediately.

Ceremonial Tools: There are these clay figures paired in 2's like Noah's Ark. They are made from an ancient kiln. I didn't remember these but I began to remember as they are shown to me. They are of animals and people. I don't recognize all the animals. Not all the animals exist anymore on earth.

Questions I asked:

Me: How do you know what animals to make for the ceremony? (as they are showing me the totems/figurines. Some are shinny and new some are old and broken looking. Some animals I recognize, some I don't. None of the animals are scary looking even the powerful ones. They all feel powerful in my hands.)

Them: The Ancient kiln tells us.

Them: (teaching me how to sit in the circle once the ceremony starts) Each person sits gently on her chair, just like you would sit on a lily pad. Softly, gently, balanced and respectful of the energy. Hold your center.

Me: (After hearing this whole lily pad thing and imagining how I would hold Gabriella in my arms) What if Gabriella won't be still or cries during the sacred circle?

Them: Then we will all harmonize again.

(It is not something they want me to worry about. She is allowed to be a child in the circle but she will be respectful no matter because the energy is so powerful. If she gets out of whack, it's because she is telling us all something is wrong.)

Women from the circle go to different places and in different forms for a time to help reconnect and evolve the feminine. Each woman has her own purpose. There are always some women who stay behind doing this ceremony in the circle. It's our way of communicating with the feminine "in the field".

They have asked me to share this information

They trust me to share it properly, protect it and bring women back to the circle that need to be healed. We have to help each and every fragment of the feminine, to make it one complete circle again. This is not a sad or war-type thing. It is just exactly what happened for our lessons and the circle is ready to be integrated again with each woman home safe and feeling whole.

This is just my little personal perspective. I think all these ideas are really interesting. I like them. I have been pushed out of this sacred circle many times as a girl. Meaning, that part of my purpose was to evolve the feminine in the language of the girl. I have died very young in most lifetimes, I have held sacred circle as a young girl. If you take classes with me, I love to keep it all silly and light-hearted. It is hard for me to write this and not sort of be ironic and silly about the whole bit of information. I want to make commentary about balancing on a lily pad and laugh my ass off. The purpose of my initiation is to learn how to hold a circle from that place of womanly power, which is a much different thing. It is not serious, but it is not making light of things. It is deep silence, it is profound joy and it is true power and essence of the divine. They are thanking me for presenting all this information in a light and entertaining way, like a child would. I started really reading and seeing very early and doing this professionally in my early 20s. And that was important. They are not taking that hilarity and lightness away, but they are helping me add this "woman" thing to my toolbox. This is the meaning of the dream for me.

Thanks for reading. Be well. –Liliana

13 MARTHA'S LABYRINTH

I started my healing practice in my early 20's when I was pregnant with my first child. When he was 4 months old my friend, Kim, graciously hosted me at her clinic in Central Oregon. She introduced me to her community as an intuitive reader. The first time I went my mother drove me and my son 3 hours into the town of Madras. My mother read the sign and said, "Ah, see, We are in the place of mothers. This is a great place for you to start."

She took care of my baby so I could spend two days working with clients. She cooked us soup and made sure I kept my strength up. She was an exceptional caretaker.

I was excited to work with the community and I was also caught up in the stereotypes of boondocks people on farms who wouldn't be open to my spiritual stuff. I was scared I would be rejected by these down-to-earth folk. What a naive woman I

was at the time and what an amazing way to dissolve the stereotype. The short of it is that people
who live away from the city actually live on the
earth, therefore they are spiritual in the most prac-
tical ways. People who tend animals and farms are
aware of the earth and connected to it because
they have to work with mother earth to grow things
and keep them alive. They are spiritual because they
are in nature. The earth is not a far-off concept.
They don't leave a 40 story building after a day's
work and drive in a car for 45 minutes to find trees.
They don't **GO** to earth, they live on it. They believe in magic. And it's ordinary everyday magic. It's
putting seeds in the earth and shit grows. It's baby
animals in the spring. It's hard fucking work and not
forgetting the seasons and emotions of weather because you just can't. They talk to the sky and pray
for it to hold back the rain until the hay gets
stored in the barn.

I began my sessions with lots of explaining, hand-
holding and apologizing. I felt unsure of myself.
They watched me squirm and kindly helped me realized my prejudice. Farmers showed up late for their

sessions because a calf decided to be born right when they were about to leave. They invited me to their homes. Fed me. Traded me for sessions with fresh produce or animal meat. They helped me build my confidence and allowed me to be green, honoring my youth and lack of experience. However they knew the value of having a energy doctor come to them regardless of my experience. They didn't hold the judgements I did.

One of my first clients was a man who looked like the Marlboro man. I was amazed at his ability to heal what I was pointing out to him in our session. Yet, when I opened my eyes, I saw a calm Marlboro man, no expression and no words. He was cool and placid as a lake. He gave nothing away. Swimming in my own anxiety, I finally asked if he was aware of the work he was doing. He answered while tugging on his belt, "Yes, Ma'ma! I can feel that from my belt buckle up." Wow! These cowboys rock! He was polite and he was so conscious of what he was doing. All I needed to do was ask.

One of the most amazing people I met was a woman named Martha Ahern. She was a beautiful earthy woman in her 50's, silver haired with a warm face. Her laugh was a playful chuckle that turned into a head-thrown-back hearty laugh. Her joy was big, and her pain was honest and raw. She offered her home for me to stay in while I worked. It was filled with stones and gems, and figurines and drums. In her backyard was a hand-built stone labyrinth. The earth spoke to her one day and, the rocks asked to be placed in a spiral and once she got moving she realized that she was building a labyrinth. A rustic-and-rugged earthy labyrinth made of stones. This was my first introduction to a labyrinth. A labyrinth that she built with stones and by hand. She has participated in MANY healing circles and she brings the wisdom of her own healing into this circle.

A labia-rinth is what I like to call it. You can create a labyrinth with anything. Laying yarn in a spiral or river stones. It doesn't actually take much space or thought. But the power is big. The walk of the labyrinth is symbolic of the path we walk in life.

The Ancient Women's Circle Dream was transformational. It came complete with instructions. When I realized that I was going to start the circle I felt ill-equipped. So I called on Martha Ahern for guidance. She lovingly coached me with a gentle hand, as I tried to get her to take on leading a circle. She chose to participate but didn't want to lead.

After my dream share: Some women said the information was familiar to them, others said that they had once had a similar dream but couldn't remember it fully. What surprised me most were the women that spiritually asked about the dream and then dreamt their own version of it. We are experiencing a collective movement in the dream-time. It involves totem animals and a sense of feminine power and healing.

ANCIENT WOMEN'S CIRCLE FACILITATOR HANDBOOK

Lotus Lantern Healing Arts

Rev. Liliana Barzola

Part story and part instruction, this is intended to be a build your own adventure guide. The notes are here the flow is yours to build.

ANCIENT WOMEN'S CIRCLE FACILITATOR HAND-BOOK

TABLE OF CONTENTS

1 FEMININE ARCHETYPES OF THE CIRCLE

"Find a place inside where there's joy, and the joy will burn out the pain."
-Joseph Campbell

For me, one of the strongest elements of the dream was experiencing the female archetypes. Seeing women own their purpose and skill was powerful. In my private practice, women sit before me asking about their "purpose" or "path in life". I almost always pull these out and start looking at their core archetype. When I know my strength and purpose, then I am much more likely to shine.

For example, as a Seer/ Storyteller, the worst thing a person could do to me is say, "I'm upset but I'm not telling you why." For me, missing information is like being stuck in an oxygen-deprived container. Information, seeing, reading, asking, learning are all the things that make life possible for me. Knowledge sustains me. I want to know EVERYTHING.

On the flip side, I am a terrible Gardener. I need Gardeners in my life. Gardeners are amazing at organization. My friend, Alethea, organizes spaces for a living. She walks right into my home and, in 30 seconds, assesses and rearranges it all in her mind. She can do the macro and micro for function and style. She is also resourceful. You don't want to spend any money? No problem, she'll repurpose something from your attic. Gardeners run companies, complex organizations and can organize the shit out of your kitchen. They are master gardeners. They are tenders.

Healers are those women who have lived through it all and they are still standing strong. They nurture. They have immense depth to them. It's the woman with the demolished heart who hums happily in her kitchen as she makes you fresh bread. They have tremendous energy for the sick and those in need. They just don't quit. If you know one, you are blessed. They are fierce lovers and protectors.

Artists make everything beautiful and they have a passion to bring the ethereal world into our three dimensional structure. I think Artists have it the hardest because they are the most self-focused of all the archetypes and we live in a society that looks down on a woman who is self-focused and driven. These women are sometimes seen as bad mothers because they choose to paint, sing, act and dance instead of tending to their kids and people. Maybe they don't get the laundry done. Maybe their kids are a bit late to school. I get mad at a friend for taking the last piece of pie without asking but then I remember she's an Artist and it just makes me smile. She's surely going to go off and write a poem about my pie.

Ancient Woman Archetypes

Some women are the GrandMothers (protectors of all of us and the information),

Some are the Artists (they make the tools for ceremony and much more)

Some are Seers (the story tellers and readers)

Some are Healers (laying on of hands and touching things to bring them back to life)

Some are called the Gardeners- (Guardians of the animals and the plants) these women are taking direct care of real animals in the barn they rotate in and out of the circle.

Some women are Seers (the story tellers and readers), She is a seeker first. Always seeking answers and experiences. She questions and is a diligent detective. She asks. Seekers look into the light and become seers and oracles. A seer is hungry for truth. They desire integrity, wisdom, vision, acceptance, expression and sensitivity. Seeing is a balancing act for them because they must release the projections of their own ego or agenda to see the truth. A seer must be willing to see all facets of themselves. For them, insight is for growth, not just information. They must look at themselves through the lens of information for transformation. Historically, they have been held responsible for what they have seen. Seers have been persecuted for knowing truth and have been hiding their purpose. They can be cold, detached, clear, objective. They are truth-seers and truth tellers. A seer strives to look and accept the truth, whether or not they like or agree with it. This is their meditation, their practice and their spiritual challenge.

Some women are the Artists (they make the tools for ceremony and much more). The Artist sees and feels the dimensions of life that are unseen by others. Her mystical vision transcends the "average" views people have of life. She experiences aspects of people, places and things on a multi-dimensional level. She hears, sees, taste, smells, feels and intuits. She has access to the stories and information in the collective in a rather organized way. What sets her apart from a Seer is her undeniable purpose to manifest the unseen dimension into physical form. Artists bring the astral-dream-time into the physical realm. The medium she uses is irrelevant. She is called to give the "subtle voice" form and texture. Unlike the Seer, she must use her personal view, passion and influence to create. As she breathes life into the immaterial, her material creation inspires others. The Artist steps into her truest communion with God when she is creating and manifesting. Things that are just out of her reach inspire her to grow and stretch. She knows how to bring essence into expression and physical form. The realm she communes with is one that we all know. Her work helps us to remember it too.

Some women are the Healers (laying on of hands and touching things to bring them back to life). The Healer is drawn to vulnerability and need in people and places. She has experienced the deepest suffering and pain imaginable. She has represented the feminine when it was being tortured and raped. Her loss and pain has not destroyed her but she has come close to death many times. She has been pushed to such a degree that nothing and no one could come to her aid but herself and the Divine. In this moment, she transformed herself by pushing beyond what was possible into a realm of divine healing. The power she gained allows her eternal access to ancient healing information. She uses this healing information in service to others. She can speak to the pleasure and joy of being female and the darkness. She understands the endurance it has taken the feminine to stay alive this long and she teaches us to respect the power and healing of the Goddess. She invokes the power of the Goddess to bring things back to life and her power is touch.

Some women are called the Gardeners (Guardians of the animals and the plants) these women are taking direct care of real animals in the barn they rotate in and out of the circle.

The Gardener embodies patience, foresight and hard work. She is a keeper and protector of people, animals, places and information. She is both a gardener and a guardian. Her sense of purpose comes from having a garden to tend to. She is always willing to destroy or remove individual parts to save the whole. Gardeners have traveled the physical and spiritual worlds. They have seen and know the darkness that exists. Gardeners have become overwhelmed, discouraged and disillusioned. In her wisdom, she has discovered that her true power comes from tending her own garden. To do this, she focuses on what she already has and moves to expand and strengthen it. Gardeners strive to make the most of their environment and resources. She looks within to find meaning and new realms of study and interest.

What is my garden? What garden is the most fulfilling to tend?

A GARDENER is someone who is drawn to care for animals, children, spaces, businesses and organizations. They move things around to make them more functional. They can decipher the needs of the garden. Gardeners are compelled to TEND by creating functional systems that support the garden. Keeping the plants watered, the animals and kids fed...the garden becomes their mission. The gardener does not own the garden. They feel whole when they have a "place" to tend. Once the garden is tended to, they rest and explore. Whether they tend a piece of property, a domain, a region, village or organization, they look holistically at all the layers of the space and the animals, people or concepts that live there. They can tend to many aspects but remain focused on the whole.

What is the story? Am I discerning the story from my own?

SEERS COMMUNICATE. They see and know the entire world like it is one big story. They read the layers of everything. Layers of energy and information. Because to them that is all there is. To them, structure is just information waiting to be read. Their challenge is to not get too personally involved with the information, otherwise they loose perspective. If you are going to get massive amounts of information, you need to process it all with neutrality. Seers feel most frustrated when they cannot receive messages. They feel stuck when their inner communication is slow or too quiet. They love being tapped into a direct line of information. They are most at peace when they are in a flow of consciousness.

What form should I take? Am I expressing myself freely?

Artists **CREATE** and **MANIFEST**. They feel passionate, impatient, full of potent expression. They get frustrated when they cannot manifest. They need to manifest, whether it is a small drawing or Fortune 500 company. Artists decipher messages from the ether and then are compelled to create an expression of that energy. Their personal involvement is vital to the creation. They are most at peace when they are creating, bringing information to life.

With what healing vibration am I most in affinity? Where will this vibration have the most impact?

Healers are **GRACEFUL MOTION.** Healers hold space for the planet. They can hold space for the sick, ill, damaged energy and people. They can get blood and guts on them because they are so focused on the healing part. The mud doesn't stick. They are committed to staying in the flow of divine healing, as this moves through them the vibration, washes the blood away. Stagnation is their Kryptonite. When the flow stops, they feel they will die. They are constantly aware of vibrations and motion. Even when they are resting deeply, they sense the healing vibrations that create rest. They are most at peace when they are in movement.

2 FACILITATING AND LEADERSHIP

"It is a curious thing, Harry, but perhaps those who are best suited to power are those who have never sought it. Those who, like you, have leadership thrust upon them, and take up the mantle because they must, and find to their own surprise, that they wear it well."
— J.K. Rowling

Maybe you have a burning desire to lead circle or maybe you just want to be a part of a circle.

Either way this chapter is designed to help you decide if leading is for you.

Leading means you set the venue, the budget, create the invitation and you use this book to guide and inspire your rituals. The guidelines and rituals in this manual provide the framework for leadership. This keeps everyone safe. There really is no need to control it. The perimeters get set and then within that container, the magic happens. The women bond, they release pain, they transform. Community is built. Being a good leader means knowing your strengths and weaknesses and that you delegate and ask for help. You are a facilitator, but also a participant. This means you let someone else cook, share, sing, tone and contribute. Sometimes emotions get intense and the energy gets too thick. When this happens you tone and revisit the guidelines. Then the energy smooths out and the laughter resumes.

If you choose to not go it alone as the leader, you can choose a co-lead. Co-leading comes with its pros and cons. On the one hand, the fantasy is that you will have a helper and a cohort to help it all go smoothly. That works if the leaders compliment each other and clearly define their individual scope. In my experience, you have to trust and admire your co-leader or it won't work. If you have a sinking feeling about your co-lead, then pay attention. Don't dismiss your natural intuition.
I did that once and I learned a lot about not listening to my gut. I was scared to lead my very first healing workshop. So out of fear, I reached out to a friend with the same mentor as me. My friend was tremendously confident. I thought this would be

great. We would split the content down the middle and I wouldn't have to go it alone.

Our planning sessions were magical and, when the time came to start the class, I realized that 90 percent of the students who signed up were my clients. Almost none of her clients joined. Those people were really there to work with me and she had no real rapport with them. That's not a problem with a leader who can read the room and match the energy of the group before diving in. Sadly, my co-leader forged ahead, talking incessantly for almost the entire session with no ability to read the room. My gut flared up in response to her disregard for the students needs. I tried a couple times to re-direct or intercept. She left about fifteen minutes for me at the end. She was grinning from ear to ear, feeling content at the workshop's finish. I could see how totally exhausted and annoyed everyone was. When you are loosing a group, you need to ask the group questions and get them involved. I could see there was no room in their brains for more in-formation, so I went around the room and cleared everyone's space and they were all glowing. Each one of them gushed, telling my how much better they felt. At the end of class, everyone was around me giving me accolades and asking me when I was teaching the next class. After everyone left, she accused me of trying to show her up. I was dumb-founded. There are times when two people are on such totally different planets there really is no room for working together. I decided to just move forward and tell her that maybe we should just teach our own classes from here on out. Later that week, our mentor scolded me. My co-leader had done an entire session on how hurt she was by "mean Liliana". She said that I fucked up our class because I went around the room healing everyone and giving my energy away. I laughed at my teacher and said, "Yeah, I know why you are reprimanding me. You want me to let people do their own work and not have me do it for them. However, after my co-leader exhausted them, I couldn't add anything but some nonverbal healing. Did she tell you that it was a 2 hour class and she talked incessantly until the last 15 minutes?"

Just because someone is more confident than you doesn't mean they are a good leader. So do a light try out before you commit to co-facilitating. When you find a natural pairing, it will be so worth it. I have had some amazing co-leaders and the high af-ter a successful circle lasts for weeks!

Also, every mistake I've made has been a powerful lesson. Don't be afraid to fail and it's okay to be transparent when you need help from the group. I have often times turned to the group and asked for direction and help. Ask in a collaborative way and it will be always be a success.

3 VENUE

"One of the deepest longings of the human soul is to be seen."
-John O'Donohue

The venue is one of the most important parts of circle.

The main reason is that it must feel safe, like a nest for the participants. Strangers may, by accident or clear intent, interrupt the circle. They are unconsciously drawn (they don't even know why) to the circle and want to join in for healing. That much potent feminine healing is like a neon spotlight in a dark cityscape. It's important that you are prepared, relaxed and unafraid.

If this occurs, I encourage you to be flattered and escort the interloper out of the space and continue your circle time. This is a sacred space for the women (or anyone who identifies as woman) in this circle to recharge. It is important that you notice that the stranger has come for healing and that you protect the space by causally walking the person back out. They do not belong there.

I was invited to a women's circle of 12 amazing Cudanderas (Latina healers). They asked me to come and do healing for them at a certain point in their group ritual. My son and his father were waiting at the neighborhood park while I worked there. At a certain point, his father came to the house with my son. Suddenly, there was this man on the porch peering in. I got up and backed him out of the space. I thought it was so interesting that he couldn't wait the full time before he began wandering into the circle. The women were calm but it was unsettling to see a strange man peering in on such a moment of intimacy. When I explained what a sacred moment this was for the women and asked him what he was doing, he couldn't explain why he showed up early.

Another time, I was hosting a women's circle deep in the basement of a wellness center. It was a professional center with lots of rooms and plenty of space between us and a busy street. While we were deep in meditation and toning, a drug-addicted man came into the room. All of the women were stuck in a moment of paralysis and shock. How could a

stranger pop into the deep recesses of the building?
How did he find us? Even on a bad day, someone
this disturbed wouldn't even make it past the front
desk, let alone the inner sanctuary. He was more
freaked out than we were. He threw his hands up
and yelled, "sorry!"

As the host of a circle, I try to position myself in
the most powerful spot in the room. I do this for
exactly these moments. I quickly got to my feet and
walked him out of the room, closing the door behind
me. I introduced myself and asked him how I could
help. As we walked out of the building together, he
explained he was looking for a drug detox center on
this street. The center was not anywhere near
where we were, but his spirit was drawn to the
healing of the circle. I redirected him politely and
he left. But I carefully and purposefully walked him
completely away. The women were worried for me
and it was sweet. I felt super present and calm. I
felt that way because I was prepared. I knew to be
flattered and I invited them to be flattered, too.

"See how powerful you are? Even people in deep
need can find you with no address. And still this is
your time. They are not welcome."

4 CONTAINERS

"We do not need magic to change the world. We carry all the power we need inside ourselves already: We have the power to imagine better."

– J.K. Rowling

Women are the containers for life.

We grow life and projects. Our families assume we will carry the energy for them. It is an automatic thing and usually involuntary. We don't even realize what we doing the carrying.

In the Ancient Woman Circle, we avoid using our bodies for this.

We use other things as containers.

For instance, a journal is a container. Writing your thoughts and emotions into the container of a journal is a powerful way to deposit the energy somewhere else.

A cup is a vessel. Holding a cup of tea is nourishing. Sometimes, I use a big, beautiful Tibetan singing bowl in the circle. I remind the ladies that this can hold the energy so they don't have to. The room is a container. I use volcanic rock as a container. A piece of obsidian in our hands does the trick. It's like a magnet taking all the excess energy and recycling it. This rock has seen the hottest, deepest darkest temperatures of the earth. Therefore, it has information for us that we need. Especially for those of us who have felt scorched by life. What is left behind is this beautiful, black rock with smooth beautiful flecks reflecting light.

When the energy feels too big, we use the cup, the journal, the rocks, the room and Tibetan bowl as reminders that we are not the containers for others. We house our own story. We house our spirit and our self-love. Everything else can go. Movement is also a big help. If a woman can move, the energy in her being and body, her body will not take on other people's workbook pages.

5 THE MEDICINE OF THE LABYRINTH

"I'll paint you moments of gold, I'll spin you
Valentine evenings..."
— David Bowie

The labyrinth is a symbol of life. It is a story of our path from birth to death, and beyond. A spiral is the simplest kind. The initiation of the circle begins with the creation of the labyrinth and each woman is a point on that spiral. There are very simple ways to create it. Usually, we take a giant roll of yarn and we have each woman hold onto it and we begin to spiral until it forms. Then each woman places a rock, shell or something earthy down where she is standing to hold her spot in the circle and the yarn stays to hold the structure of the spiral. Sometimes, we write words on the rocks that we place in the labyrinth. The word can be an intention, a fun word, or a word that you want to leave behind.

What happens when you are trying to move forward and can't see your path ahead?

This is the Medicine of the Labyrinth. A story about navigating in the dark from Martha Ahern.

Martha was the one who helped me understand the power of the labyrinth. I had the honor of getting to walk a stone labyrinth she built by hand. Martha would drive three hours drive from Central Oregon to Portland to come and join us in the circle. She had to wake up early, when it was still dark outside. Before she got into her car, she always felt compelled to walk the labyrinth in the dark, like she would be bringing us it's good juju. She laughed at the craziness of walking the stone labyrinth in the dark. Still, she did it. It was tricky avoiding the stones and rocks that made up the labyrinth. She explained, "Sometimes we can't make out directions, we fumble around in the dark, we can't tell what is up and what is down. Then a passageway like the labyrinth shows up. There are two directions: one is forward and one is back." She laughed heartily as she provided it as a metaphor for life. So many times, we are walking our path in the dark.

Rarely in life do we know what is ahead of us on the path, but we certainly know what is behind us.

We think, "I've been there, done that. I closed the door to that past. The door is shut so I can move forward." Even still, there are those moments of doubt or fear when we check to see if the door to the past will still open for us; whether we are feeling co-dependent, nostalgic or taunting ourselves with the pain from the past. Sometimes, I have found myself banging on that fucking door and begging to be let back in. When the door doesn't open and the panic subsides, I realize there is only forward for me. I find relief after the panic. But not usually for some time.

6 THE CIRCLE DOES IT ALL

Today, I am sitting in the fullness of my newest circle of women. It is our closing circle. It takes so much faith, trust and energy to get me to this weekend. Well worth it, as twenty-four exquisitely beautiful, unique, wise women, ages 18-67, have been initiated. I continue to learn so much about magic and trust. I set the stage and steer the ship, but their stories and beauty create the vessel. I am humbled by each one of them. Each time, I have to trust the process.

There is so much collective feminine pain. When you facilitate this type of group, it is powerful and it changes you and the world. As each individual woman releases and transforms her pain, it, in turn, inspires healing for those around them. This is something that the women usually mention after the first day. They realize they are clearing trauma from the collective feminine essence.

Women often carry the persecution of the feminine essence through past lives and even from our genetic lineage.

It takes courage to do this work.

Not every woman is ready for it, and that is okay. I have found that I rarely have to turn women away who are not ready because they talk themselves out of it. Be it time issues or monetary commitment. The bottom line is that a woman has to have the space in their hearts and lives to do this circle. There was one woman in the first round who was not ready and I ignored that. I denied it. Yet she kept telling me and I kept encouraging her and telling her it was fine. There is a difference between encouraging someone that they can be their diverse and unique self and convincing someone to join because you felt they need the healing so desperately. And that is what I did. I didn't truly honor that her excuses were about not being ready and I wanted to love her through it. Not helpful in the end. My denial just made her spin out like a top. It was too much and she continued to make excuses about why someone else should take her place in the group. I got tired half way through the year supporting her and encouraging her to stay. What a powerful lesson for me in learning to honor someone else's limits.

So if a lady is not ready, listen to her. If a woman is like, "I feel so called! I heard your first two sentences and I was like, yes! Finally!", that is the right time for her. If she follows with confusion, needs clarification on what this group is about, then communicate it and back off. The women of a developing circle will magically call each other in without your manipulation or will. The women in your invisible community are making you read this book. They are encouraging you to start it. They will dialog in the dream time, configure and reconfigure until each one makes it to the initiation.

For example, sometimes a woman will join and say, "Do you have women in the group who like to garden? I would really like a friend to garden with." I get to say, "I don't know just yet, but if you feel committed to the circle you can make that request from spirit now. Just call her in." In my experience, that is what will happen. Women will shuffle around until the perfect balance is created.

I encourage diversity in age, culture, color, expression; all of it is needed. I don't usually let anyone younger than sixteen join in. The circle can be intense sometimes. There are exceptions of course. Women who have never done something like this before are, of course, always welcome. There are no spiritual requirements to be in circle.

7 USE & DISCLAIMER

These guidelines are to be used solely as a tool during planning and implementation of your very own Ancient Women's Circle. By no means is the information or the guidelines and instructional outlines provided to be used without also implementing professional judgment. If you are someone who plans to use this material to further your own offerings, we request that you credit Rev. Liliana Barzola with creation of this format and the material herein. Lotus Lantern Healing Arts, the author, and all advisors on this project accept no liability whatsoever for any injuries to persons or property resulting from the application of the practices implied in this facilitators manual.

8 TEN MONTH COMMITMENT

You can hold circle however you like.
I recommend a 10 month journey, just like gestation.
It gives the group time to grow and bond. I recommend you meet at least three times in-person and do some phone or email support.

Here is what my invitation looks like:

Women are coming together with healthy boundaries (no drama, no saccharine and no competition) to create a space for the feminine to heal. A creative space will be built. A safe space is opening and we are the creators and weavers of this healing path. The Ancient Women's Circle is a 10-month commitment to yourself. Support and healing is offered to you as you access the divine feminine within. Through meetings, both virtual and in person, you will have the opportunity to create connections with other phenomenal women. For a whole year, this community can provide support for you as you blossom. This journey is lead by Rev. Liliana Barzola, who will provide coaching and guidance for you throughout the year.

This Ancient Women's Circle was remembered by Liliana and she is being instructed by the "Grand-Mothers" to share the dream and re-create the circle earth-side. As we re-center ourselves in this Ancient Women's Circle, each one of us has an opportunity to access the guidance and messages within it.

Why the costs?
You are welcome to take the dream and make it yours. Dream your own dream and create your own healing for the year at no cost. The money you pay into it provides us the funds to have a healing space to do this work. Rent, overhead, facilitating, planning, processing.

You will begin tracking your nighttime dreams, labyrinth building, journaling, communing with other women and understanding your divine feminine archetype.

What does the commitment truly mean?

It means you will join us for the weekend initiation. All other meetings are optional. You can decide after this meeting how deeply you want to get into this process. You can move forward and complete the year on your own, or you can join us for the virtual and in-person meetings.

YOU DECIDE after our first connection what your next step is.

ALL WOMEN WHO FEEL CALLED ARE WELCOME TO JOIN US!

Pass it along.

Understanding Virtual Tuesday Night Monthly Meetings.

I selected the virtual meetings because we are all busy. The meetings will be just a small check in. We will have an opportunity to share. As you know, 20 some women sharing takes a long time. :) So I might give you a set amount of time to share. The "Share" is an opportunity for you to talk about your month, your process, the GrandMothers Balancing Ritual, a dream you had...It is up to you. The GrandMothers have asked that we meet in person around the seasonal transitions; summer, fall, winter.

9 APPLICATION

Application for the Ancient Women's Circle

We want to create a balanced and cohesive group of women.

Please help us understand who you are by filling out this application. After your application is reviewed, we will set up a time to chat with you. Thank you for your interest in the circle and for taking the time to apply. Your responses will be kept confidential.

QUESTIONS:

What is awesome about you? What do you love about yourself?

How did you hear about this circle?

Have you worked with the (host/hosts) before?

Have you participated in a women's group before? If so, describe your experience.

What are your expectations for this circle? How do you see it helping you?

Do you currently have a support system? If so, describe?

Have you experienced betrayal from women in the past? Do you have trust issues with women? Share as much as you feel comfortable with.

Describe what it might feel like/what it feels like to have healthy women in your life?

Are you comfortable with the idea of toning, humming or singing in a group?

Choose the questions that feel relevant to you and answer as many as you like:

1. What are you excited about at this moment?
2. When was the last time you felt inspired?
3. If you could be in your dream place at the moment, what would you be doing?
4. What's been tempting you lately?
5. What's been the one most consistent thing in your life?
6. What gives you butterflies in your tummy?

10 NOURISHING THE CIRCLE

Nourishing the circle with the ritual of food, beverages and snacks is vital to the circle.

Group meals offer a moment to step away from processing and holding space to really nourish the body, regulate blood sugar and share in a much more natural way.
The focus is on the meal. It's the lunch bell ringing in class and there is a shift in energy, an exhale.

You probably know the fable of Stone Soup.
A stranger enters a village and offers to make a community meal. A pot of boiling water is made and the stranger adds a stone. Each person adds something; onions, potatoes, scraps from their kitchens. At the end of the day, everyone eats a delicious soup. I have found this IS the best way to feed a group.

We arrive in the morning with enough crock pots to make the soup, no stove top required. Women bring a little something to add to the soup. Sending out a grocery list of ideas is a great start. A little onion, some garlic, different veggies and fresh herbs. I usually bring some chicken thighs to add and lots of lemon and salt, as well. It has always worked out with out having to control the process. Each pot can be a different theme, gluten free or vegetarian. Women stand around cutting things and adding things together. It's wonderful to have a Healer or Artist take the lead on cooking. The pots are filled and left to cook as the group session starts. Usually the soup's mouthwatering scent drifts into circle preciously at the lunch hour. We usually add some artisan bread, seasonal fruit and make a salad. It creates a really nourishing flow. And it's a free catered lunch. Warming things like tea and ciders are really great additions too!

11 SINGING & TONING

I have to admit that I've been keeping something from you.

I've done it because I fear rejection. I was afraid if I started out telling you this, that you would most likely be singing in this group... you wouldn't have read this far.

So if you are like me and you do not consider yourself a songstress, let me explain before you run away. There is almost always someone in the group that is brave enough and comfortable enough to take up this post. As a non-singer, I have found that toning and singing are profoundly healing for the group.

We use sound to heal the space. We do this so the women do not become sick by processing their sisters toxicity. When sitting in a group, there is a natural tendency to empathically take on other people's energy, pain and stories. We do this because we have a matching picture, a similar experience, and it reminds us of something. So the energy doesn't stagnate in the room, we use sounds.

After a woman shares, we all tone for a moment. We hold an "Aaaaaahhhhh" or "Oooooohhhh" sound. If her story makes us emotional, we resist the temptation to fix or heal or share our own story. We are remain silent. Committed to holding space. We let the room do the work of being the container. Then, when she is finished sharing, we tone. I recommend using a singing bowl or a chime to start you off. The woman concludes her share and someone hits the bowl and we all tone. The women might do this for one breath or a couple times over. Either way the group will know what to do. It will feel right.

Feels amazing. It's a way to move the energy and release for a new beginning.

12 BRING YOUR ELDERS

It is important to remember those that have paved the way for us. Our elders have wisdom to share. Daily communion with the GrandMothers in meditation is powerful. If you know a living GrandMother, ask her questions. Take in her vantage point. If they are safe, if they are healthy, then invite them into your life. Learn from them. I ask the women to bring something to represent their elders. Bring the photos of your grandmothers or anyone that you admire as a guardian, passed or present.

For me it's Angela Lansbury, my Abuelita, my Mother and Sister.

Who is it for you?

13 STRESS FREE SUPPLY LIST

(FOR PARTICIPANTS)

This is supposed to be 100% free, so if you start stressing, just move to the next thing on the list.

-Pillow

-Blanket

-Journal and Pen

-Water bottle and snacks

-Something to add to the stone soup

-Something you are ready to pass on. Maybe it's an old necklace or a shell you found on the beach. Look around your home for a trinket that you cherished at one point but now you feel ready to pass it on to someone else.

-A picture of an elder or something that represents GrandMother for you.

-Anything else you need to help you feel comfortable.

14 THE NIGHT BEFORE

I invite the women to the venue the night before the initiation.

This should be done at night when the veil is thin, the day is done and the women are a bit more relaxed. Attendance is **NOT** mandatory. The initiation is considered to happen the next morning. This is a chance for the women to create the space together ahead of time and so you aren't caught up in perfecting everything for them for the next day. This makes it really feel like a community.

Start somewhere around 4:00pm

Remind the women that we agree to maintain an emotionally safe, open-minded space. This space is sacred and so is our time together. Honoring the women in the space means honoring yourself.

Give a casual tour around the venue and discuss where to put things. It's a fun opportunity to set it all up beforehand and step into the space fresh the following morning. You can basically Pintrest the shit out of the night before!

You will create:

1. Meeting Space For Sharing (enough space for everyone in the group to be in one place)

2. Labyrinth Area

3. Sacred Obsidian Site. This represents the center of the Earth, a place women can go off and process if they need to. We usually have some pillows and blankets to relax on, a bowl of salt with tea lights (some representation of fire) and obsidian rocks. This spot is the magnet that soaks up the garbage you are letting go of.

4. Tea Apothecary (tea, cups and water)

5. Altar For The GrandMothers. We create an altar for the Grandmothers. In this altar, we add pictures of loved ones, figurines and trinkets. We also think of this as a place for the women who couldn't come, are late or are missing. It's place for the women who have passed on/ancestors to be remembered.

6. Some Solo Sites (spots where people can go and write or meditate alone or separately)

Ask the group questions like:

Where we should we make the labyrinth?

Where do the put an alter for the Grandmothers? Tea apothecary? Snooze room? Circle gathering? Food?

What shall we use to decorate the space?

If you are freaking out right now ("I don't have room for all that!")... don't worry! You can make it work. I have done circles in small spaces and we just do a "set change".

15 GUIDELINES

Share the guidelines upfront, either in the invitation to the group or the moment we come together to participate. This makes expectations clear. When the circle begins, we discuss the guidelines even before introductions. This provides the participants a moment to check in with whether or not they still want to participate.

How we handle someone breaking a guideline is by reminding them what the guideline is. If someone breaks a guideline, we assume they are struggling and just need a reminder. In the dream, the Grand-Mothers modeled this. The reminder is firm but not shaming or condescending. Leaders can break a guideline and it's okay to self-forgive and reset and try again. Be honest about it and let other women provide feedback. There is no need to be harsh. We are learning how to be healthy in a group. This means letting go of a lot of family dysfunction that we unconsciously harbor but that comes up to the surface during group. Toning will help with this a lot.

A note about sharing: The host picks a direction to begin the sharing; either clock wise or counter clockwise. As you come to a participant always ask if she wants to share. There is no pressure to share. She says either yes or no. If she says yes, she shares and everyone tones for her after her share then we move to the next woman. If she says no, you move to the next person. Once the entire circle has been asked and completed, the women who have chosen not to share, are given one more opportunity. It is a courtesy to ask at the end in case something has changed for them. Still there is no expectation to share!

Ancient Women's Circle Guidelines:

Circle participation means agreement to the following guidelines:

No one is ever made to feel fearful.

Everyone is sacred.

Everyone is here because they are important.

Everyone who is here is here because they want to be here.

The concept of "obligation" is irrelevant. Everyone has a purpose.

Like a symphony each woman has her own unique purpose.

Competition does not exist in this space. It is not even a concept.

Confidentiality: We keep stories and experiences of our sisters sacred and safe.

We take responsibility for our individual needs. This means speaking up. Ask for what you need instead of hoping or assuming the circle will know and respond appropriately.

Circle sharing means listening without agenda.

Speaking and listening from our hearts.

Speak from our own experiences rather than speaking for each other.

We listen with discernment instead of judgment.

We are committed listeners, honoring each other's experiences. We offer no advice, fixes or problem solving. We allow our sisters' their opinions, feelings, disappointments and growth periods. We accept each other as we are.

This is **OUR** circle.

Keep your hands to yourself while a woman is in her process. If a woman is in her grief or pain, she may tremble or cry. Do not touch her unless she initiates or asks for physical support. You may disturb her natural process of healing.

The purpose of the circle:
To Bring Balance Within Ourselves and Within the Universe through sight and telling stories.
To Share and Support Each Other.
To Gather Information (by reading energy and remembering).
To Protect the Animals.

The Containers / Bowl

You are a vessel, a container. You hold energy within you. Your body and heart are magic. Your womb and cervix and pelvic bowl hold energy, too. Sometimes, the energy is too big for us to hold or contain. In these moments, we need a container. Containers available to you are your journal, the framework and center of the labyrinth, and the sacred obsidian sites. Use these spaces to process and let these things hold what you cannot. All of these places lead to the center of the earth. Mother Earth is connected to you through your grounding. She is your Mother, she and the GrandMothers will hold you and accept you always.

16 WHAT HAS DEVASTATED YOU

Devastation is a big, scary word.

Here we get right to the core of what has shaped you. I don't know a wise woman who hasn't experienced deep heartache, a devastating pain, or a dark night of the soul that seems to go on forever and never let up.

When I asked a woman in circle, "What has been the most consistent thing in your life?" she answered, "My ability to overcome pain. I will not say that pain is constant, but I have had a great deal of it. My perseverance has allowed me to grow and become the person that I am."

(Journal, Share and Tone)

17 INITIATION WEEKEND

If a woman cannot make it to every gathering or meeting, that is okay!

However, to be a part of the circle you **MUST** attend the initiation.

The initiation forges the circle into being. It is disruptive when a participant joins in later; even special guests are experienced as interlopers.

This journey begins with an initiation into the sacred women's circle. The purpose of this journey is to build a community of conscious women that support each other. Each participant brings their unique experience and each one of us is sacred.

The Ancient Women's Circle is a space:

- Where women come together
- Where you are asked to self-care (that means putting yourself first)

- To support and maintain healthy boundaries
- To welcome the feeling of being loved, accepted, inspired.
- To let your authentic self shine

Saturday:

Arrive for tea and treats. Chat a bit.

Take our seats in the circle.

Cast the Circle:

"From the power of the elements, earth, air, fire and water... from the guardians of the directions eagle, coyote, bear, owl and all the animal totems from the spirit of transformation and integration, we call upon the ancient ones; the GrandMothers who watch, protect, guide, direct and support us on our journey. Welcome! Ah ho, blessed ones!"

– Pat Ahern

Read and Agree to the Guidelines.

Welcome! Introduce yourself and your co-facilitator (if you have one).

Basic grounding meditation

GrandMother's Meditation: Setting the intention for the space, asking the grandmothers for wisdom guidance and support.

Pick a river stone and write a word/wish on the stone.

Take the yarn and create the circle. We sing or tone while we create the labyrinth. Each woman places a stone down for herself.

Sit in circle afterwards and take your journal out.

Write the answers to these questions:

1. Why do you think you were called to this circle?

2. Why do you want to be here?

3. Why do you not want to be here?

Introductions/Greetings: Use the questions you answered.

Host explains how to deal with hard moments: Toning, sacred obsidian sites, laying down and resting, talking to the GrandMothers, journaling, getting tea.

Talk about containers that we have. Containers can hold the energy for you when the energy gets to be bigger than you. Grounding, meditation, journaling and the "fire" place, walking the labyrinth.

Allow yourself to be consciously triggered. It helps you to release the denial and guilt that the feminine essence has been holding. What to do if you are feeling critical? Understand that you are healing. Ask yourself, what does the person who is triggering me or this situation remind me of?

We invite the GrandMothers and our ancestors to heal and guide us. When you leave here, they go with you. Welcome and remember those whom have passed. Practice holding space for each other.

We walk our gift to pass on into the labyrinth. The offering will be cleansed there in the center of the labyrinth.

Purification Ritual: Ceremonial cleansing. Clearing the old pain, fear and limiting agreements/belief that dim our light.

What has devastated you journaling or art

Lunch 12:30pm

Share what has devastated you.

Close the day's work

Saturday Night Homework: Drink your dream tea, rest and have a bath.

Sunday:

Arrival

Restate guidelines.

Walk the labyrinth together.

Do a meditation asking the Grand Mothers for support and guidance.

Complete any sharing from the day before.

Argentine Mate Ritual: (You will need a gourd, mate and a bombilla)

Sit in the circle on the floor. The cebadora (mate brewer/host) pours the hot water into the gourd and drinks the fist cup.

Then the gourd is refilled with water and passed counter-clockwise with the bombilla (straw-filter) facing the recipient. Each person drinks the entire gourd. "You share the vessel, not the liquid."

The recipient of the gourd has as much time as needed to finish the gourd-full. After the last few

sips of the mate are gone, the gourd is returned
with the bombilla facing the cebadora. The gourd is
refilled with hot water and follows around the circle, continuing in this fashion until the mate is
lavado (flat). If someone has had enough mate, they
simply say gracias (thank you) to indicate that they
are finished. You can laugh and talk and play during
this time. It's meant to be fun.

Purification: Ceremonial cleansing. Clearing the old
pain, fear and limiting agreements/belief that dim
our light. Get rid of what is worn out or old, and to
receive what is new and fresh. Think of this as a
graduation from an old way of doing things. Step
into what can truly support you this weekend. Build
a support system. Remember, you are not alone.
There is no one like you; the beauty of that. You
express a unique aspect of the feminine that no one
else in this circle can. What would you like the sisterhood to hold space for? What dreams and wishes
are you trying to manifest?

Walk into the spiral and retrieve a gift.
Sit circle and share what you picked. Now the giver
can share who they are and the meaning that the
gift had for them. This is a magical moment when
connections are made. I find this to be one of the

most powerful rituals. It is a great example of the power of the circle. Frequently women find profound meaning in this accidental connection.

Close the circle:

"Guardians and spirits of the North/South/East/ West, our circle is now complete. Farewell, spirits of the North, Grand Mothers and Old Ones of the Earth. We thank you for your presence. 'Til the next time Mighty Ones, go in peace but protect and guide each woman as she leaves this circle. We declare this scared circle closed."

Blow out the candles.

18 GRANDMOTHER'S MEDITATION

Some women are the The GrandMothers
(the protectors of all of us and the information)

The GrandMothers are comforting, welcoming and
nurturing.
They are a circle of women in spirit.
They reside in the astral.
The GrandMothers are calm and hopeful because
they understand that healing is occurring.
They are not afraid.
They are active and available at all times.
They hold the best interest of us all within their
hearts.
The feminine essence (Yin) is growing and healing
our earth. It is creating the balance that is needed.

They are wise and have seen and lived, they have
held the yin essence and blood in their wombs. They
have the answers. They have compassion for you,
patience and limitless love. They are connected to
nature, to ancient traditions. They have been
present since the moment of your creation and know
how to guide you. They are whole and they help us

all to be whole. They initiate us into the spiritual world. In the West, we have lost our connection and the GrandMothers are here to hold the space for us as we reconnect.

Anchor completely into your body. Make sure you are connected to earth and sky.
Sit in the center of your head and look deeply into your heart.

Your heart is where the Grandmothers leave you messages.

Looking into the center of my heart (your message center). What colors do you see? I see yellow, gold, champagne and pink.

Imagine a writing desk in the center of your heart. On that desk, there is a seashell. It is a spiral. What is your special message from the GrandMothers? Maybe it is the same as mine. Maybe it is different.

If your message a feather, a leaf, a star, a strand of leather, a golden treasure. My shell is a spiral. My shell is iridescent and warm in the palm of my hand, it glows softly.

I hold it to my ear and hear the GrandMothers whispering. Reminding me to be strong, that they love me, that they know where I am. They are watching and protecting me. They are closer than I think.

I am ready to enter the Ancient Women's circle and so are you.
It is a space that is far away. It resides in the astral. It is also closer than you think. So enter with me now.

Are you climbing a spiral staircase? Are you walking deep into the earth? Are you journeying to the center of a tree? Are you sailing on a ship to a tea party?

Look at the level of protection that surrounds this ancient place. Is it a circle of boulders? Then, peak between these big rocks and see the flames of a fire making the rocks shimmer and sparkle?
Are you at the doorway of a great wall or tree? Whatever it is for you, make sure you pay careful attention to the archway as you pass through.
Is it ornate? Look at the etchings and markings on the walls. The Artists have been here. The Artists

are taking you toward the Ancient kiln. See the
fires roaring. The statues are before you, figurines
and different animal shapes. Some are large, some
small, some detailed and perfect, some crumbling.
Do you recognize these animals? See the pairs,
masculine and feminine. The ancient kiln creates us
all. The Artists are here to answer your questions.

Play for a moment with this....

Now you are walking through the barn. This barn is
a circle of stalls. It feels like there are horses inside the stalls. The scent is earthy and sweet.
Can you hear the horses making their noises and
moving around a bit.
As you walk past, notice that some horses are at
peace and some are struggling.

There are women Gardeners all around. These
women are the Guardians of the animals; they communicate with them and tend to their needs. You
are walking through an elaborate system of support.
Some Healer women are laying their hands on these
animals and healing them. You pass by some open
stalls and see the glow from the healers' hands.
Hear the animals calming to their touch. The Gardeners and Healers are working together. The

Artists are there too. They make this circular barn feel warm by tending the fires. It feels like Persia here. It feels like Asia here. It feel like the Amazon here. It feels like Africa here. It feel like Viking country, too.

The lighting is warm. This place is bright but soft. It is hard to witness the struggle in these animals. These are feminine essences that have come back from difficult places and are being healed and restored.

They are being celebrated for their hard work. They are being told to rest. Let's move deeper into the center of the barn.
Now you are moving into a room that feels like a parlor.

It feels like a warm old house with a big open room and lots of comfy places to sit. You are at the innermost center.

This is where the Grand Mothers and the Seers are. And they are humming. Can you feel the vibration as you enter this sacred space? Feel the power they yield with wisdom, kindness and knowing.

Now find your place in the circle. It is a spiral; a circle within a circle. Your sacred Grand Mothers protect you.
Snuggle into the center, if you like.
Are you floating on a lily pad or sinking into an old fashioned, comfy chair?

It is warm here. It is a respite. There is work to do, but you are not alone. You are never alone. Alone is a lie.

In this room, there are many Seers. Look around the room and notice who these women are; you know them, you may have been embodied with them now on earth, maybe they have passed away. Gardeners, Healers, Artists too.

Take a moment to look around and see who is here for you. Who is part of your sisterhood? Notice all the different personalities of these women and how that are invited to be themselves.

Some of them are knitting, some are sipping tea, some are snacking, laughing, playing chess, and making tinctures. It is not busy work just soft en-joyment.

Now sense into the feelings in this room. You may not like it, it might feel like grief, it might feel like the most intense pain you have ever felt, and it might make you feel like you are going to pass out. You are in the deepest chamber of the feminine and there is a lot of healing happening, but sometimes healing just feels like pain.

Stay with these uncomfortable emotions as long as you can. Breathe. Don't struggle. Look around at the Grand Mothers. Look into your sisters' eyes and see how much they love and support you. They are calm. They know this grief will lift and shift. They know that transformation is happening. Clarity is yours. Now sit deep in these emotions.
Now notice that they are all toning for you
Now begin to tone with them, silently, but loud within yourself.

Keep at this until you can feel your center again.
Now is your time to dialog with the GrandMothers.
Sit in this space and listen. You are safe.

19 FINDING & BALANCING

Discuss the Archetypes lightly and make a decision about which one you think you might be.

1. Meditate on your archetype.

2. Loosely write about your acceptance and resistance to it. Write down the negatives and positives of your archetype. Why **DON'T** you want to be associated with it: Fears and resistance, societal views. What will happen to you if you commit to this archetype. Why **DO** you want to be associated with it? What is positive about this archetype? What is romantic about it? What is the freedom it will bring you?

3. Ask for balance of the negative and positive aspects of your archetype. You can take a walk around your inner labyrinth or literally take a walk. You will know how to process it.

Blessing: GrandMothers, I have opened the space for healing. Give me strength and joy on this path.

Look after me as I begin to love myself on a deeper level. Gratitude.

Now share and tone in the circle.

20 FALL

Witchy Delight

This Day is Celebration and Fun

We are here to enjoy the full moon energy and each other.

Witches are women that have a connection to nature. The Earth is a pretty magical place.
So let's play with the earthly magic and celebrate our sisterhood.

1.Create the space: chairs, decor, rocks....YOU **WILL NEED A CAULDRON FOR THIS!**
2. Meditate on the wisdom of the GrandMothers and Crones.
3. Enter the spiral circle, tone and return to circle.
4. We call this ritual, "talking out of turn". Whoever feels inspired goes up to the cauldron in the center of the circle. She shouts into it everything she wants to get rid of. Releasing the old and decaying things in your life; bad self image, insults, jobs, old ways and patterns that no longer serve you. What one woman releases, she releases for the

circle. As each woman is shouting into the center, the entire group tones for her.

5. Drink tea for healing and to fortify your space. You are renewed and supported.

Homework: Full moon meditation.

Find the moon and say hello to her. She has guided you through the night for eons. Thank her for all that she does for the world and you personally. Ask the moon to take, release and transform the things that no longer serve you. Trust that she can do this and that in the morning you will begin to strengthen and nourish your inner core for this winter. You are in a deep healing that will flourish in the spring.

21 WINTER

This reconnection is going to tap into the power of support and generosity. Who are the people in your life that have held you up and what have you learned from them.
Leaving a legacy.
Bring something sparkly.

Welcome
Create a Red Tent feel for the day; blankets and pillows, decorations with twinkle lights and candles
Snacks and tea
Start by reading the guidelines and opening the circle
Enter the labyrinth with silence and begin toning
Meditation on a Power Animal and Share
Animal Cards or tarot card playing. Pulling cards for past, present and future.
Eat a meal together.

22 GRANDFATHERS MEDITATION

Call upon the Grandmothers.

Imagine a circle of Grand Fathers around you.

Are they wrinkled with strong, sun kissed faces?
Are they Yoda or Gandalf?
As you look at them, remember them and see their
palpable wisdom.

The Grand Fathers are vibrating at balanced essence of the healthy masculinity.
They are vibrating at divine knowing.
They are vibrating at picking your ass up and carrying you, kicking and screaming, while lifting boulders
out of your way.
Imagine them making a half circle of protection behind you and now turn around and face them,
choose to look at them. Some may look indigenous
and some may look like the "most interesting man"
in the world from the Dos Equis commercial.
Doesn't matter. What matters is that they are here

for us. That they harness that essence of sage, father, king and protector of you.
I want you to ask them for a gift.

Ask that a GrandFather step forward for you. That he show you how he can be a protector, offer you blessings, strength and balance.
What does he place in the palm of your hand?
He's got the plan for riding triumphantly through your pain to your success. He loves you and is over joyed to be your protector.
Call them here to you when you need council. They can talk strategy and share wisdom. They can even do some of the heavy lifting for you.

Ask the Grand Fathers to take care of all the toxic masculine vibrations on the planet. You are stepping out of this job and passing it to them. It is not your work to heal it, it never was. The Grand Fathers will take this job back now.

This is what I wrote last year at this time:
This was a particularly difficult month for me to be a co-leader. Martha couldn't make it to the circle and so it was on my already shaky shoulders. I was suffering from a yeast infection in my breast, which made nursing my baby difficult. I was really not

feeling confident in my abilities as a leader. I was
exhausted and the circle was an after thought. To
top it all off, I kept logging on the forum and seeing
how much struggling the women were feeling. They
were all in need and feeling like support was lacking
big time. I lay in my acupuncture session with a
mentor and told her how irritated I was with the
world. "Stagnant liver chi," she said. I was grumpy
as all hell. I lay there feeling overwhelmed with my
own life and fearful of letting the circle down. This
would be our first in-person meeting since the initiation. The initiation was something I spent 6 month
preparing. Getting guidance from the Grand Mothers, tasting teas, looking into journals and supplies.
Now I was entertaining ideas of nap-time for us and
somehow playing it up as all the GrandMothers
idea. Ha, ha!

My mentor pushed me to go deeper, to stop avoiding the fear of failing and to realize that, yes, in
this moment, I had zero energy and zero support to
give. Today, I was a crappy mother, my marriage
was falling apart, I was broken and maybe too sick
to even make it to the meeting. What an uncomfortable place to sit in; the grief, lack and despair.
And how wonderful it feels to accept it, give up
and stop struggling. Just taking a breath and feel-

ing my emotions without problem solving. Because this is exactly the moment that I am taking care of me, nourishing myself and restoring.

In that moment, the class was born and The Grand Mothers knew I was ready for the message.

The first couple minutes, the women settle in and we discuss the events for the day, getting logistics out of the way. We start with a 30 minute silent meditation and then we move into the labyrinth space silently. We each find the spot that feels right and, once we do, we begin toning. Some women are energetically toning and some are doing it out loud. I am reminded at the power of our vibrant voices and how we begin to sound like a choir of angels. The toning is always invigorating and calming, it's a wonderful mix. Better than a cocktail!

We sit circle again and I share my idea of feeling unsupported and what that brings up. We sit in it. I introduce Leslie Temple Thurston's technique of "polarity squares" and we do the process as a group.

We write list: Our desire for support and our desire for no support.

We discuss:
What happens when we need help and it doesn't come?
Is it difficult or easy for ask for help?
We look at the our commitment to taking care of everyone else first.
Letting go of control.
Allowing the help to come.
Going into the Archetype of the healer.
Positive and negatives of it.
What does it feel like to walk away when everything is collapsing around you?
When has that happened to you in the past or present?

23 ARCHETYPE EXPRESSION

Journal or Art: Looking at Yourself Through an Archetype.

Make a piece of artwork expressing the struggles and the joys of your archetype.

It can be a painting, drawing or a poem.

Do it with these questions in mind:

What does my archetype need to feel whole again?

What does my inner world need to feel like?

How do I want to be supported?

Share you art or gift with the group. Ask the group for agreement and support. As each woman shares what she needs and wants, listen deeply and take a moment to hold that vision and see that for her.

24 SPRING

Creating a Ceremonial Necklace for the Journey

Let's create something to physically connect you to your sisterhood.

It is a talisman of healing and support. When you put on the necklace, it provides the Grand Mothers protection and serves as a way to connect and communicate with your circle.

Gather the Artists in the group for this project. Ask for their help facilitating this and helping the women find their beads and to do the clasping or wrapping involved in the creation of this ceremonial necklace. At least one or two women are usually willing. I usually have the same pendant as the center piece, but each woman will create her own combination of beads. We found pendants that were spirals, goddesses, animals and labyrinths. We found female artists to make them.

1. Place the beads in the center of your labyrinth and let the women go choosing their beads and pendant. Spend the day creating their necklaces, asking the GrandMothers and each other for support and guidance.

2. When their piece is complete, they are invited to walk their sacred necklace into the labyrinth for a blessing. It is fun to walk through a couple times and see all the amazing pieces.

3. Eat something yummy!

4. Each woman retrieves their necklace and returns it to the circle. Following the neutral guidelines, they each have a chance to share their process in it's creation. Then she voices her wish for support to the circle.

For example: Clarity, peace, support for my new job, finding a partner, etc. Lastly, she passes the necklace around the circle as the women are toning to support for her intention.

When the necklace's owner receives her necklace back, it is filled with sisterhood magic.

25 SUMMER

Celebration of Sensuality and Sexuality.

Holistic Sexuality: The wholeness of your sensual, sexual self.

Sensuality: The sensual has to do with senses. That may have nothing to do with sex.

Throughout our lives, we have been learning to trust our body and all our sensual feelings. Sensuality is the spark of our creative energy. We live in a world that sexualizes the feminine instantly. Sometimes it's the sensual we want. Sensuality is a soothing exploration of the senses. Think delicious food, warm baths, laying in the sun or getting snuggled. Sometimes, I want to have an orgasm and "get off." These things can very often be totally different paths.

As a young woman, I wanted to understand how to please a partner. Sex was all about the other person. As I have matured, I became solidly interested in my own experience of pleasure. From belly dancing when I was 16 years old to now dancing around my living room to Paul Simon with my daughter; I love to love my body. I enjoy connecting to creative sensations and expressions.

Let's release the shame that has been imprinted upon our bodies concerning pleasure.

Sex and Sexuality:
Orgasm is a release of energy. Owning your body and your pleasure means clearing the guilt and trauma that we hold in our physical and energetic bodies. We all need clearing around this. Even if we don't have a history of sexual trauma. The guilt is built in. Also, bodies are sexualized and criticized so that we miss out on the deeper connection with our sensual selves.

Our culture is fast-paced and all about what can be achieved and accomplished. How much money can be made. It forgets about enjoyment and slowing down.

Our culture sees sex as unclean and dark. And when we want to reclaim that, we have to explain ourselves. Apologize.

There is such a thing as Holistic Sex. The Taoists understand this. They have mapped out the whole body's system of the male and female sex organs and understand that vibrant sex is part of being healthy.

For the feminine, connection and play is important in sensual and sexual experiences.

What is sensual to you?

My friend and I were recently talking about our children. She made the observation that coming of age into the sensual and sexual world felt frustratingly different for girls than for boys. She gave the example of how her sons may discover sex thru a "wet dream", accidental orgasm, or looking at someone and finding themselves aroused. But for many girls, it is often times about bleeding, and then all the maintenance that comes with that. Or breasts that are budding for all to see and have an opinion about. There is a layer of responsibility that girls becoming women have to process. That boys may not have until much later, or for some, ever. That all of the sensual and sexual feelings come with the weight of unwanted pregnancy, or the chore of moon time.

As a girl, I was angry and resistant to all this. As a woman, I have come to relish in these things and honor the ceremony around moon time. Yet, I am in a world that doesn't stop for my moon time. Where is my red tent?

Journal: Remember back to the time your were becoming a woman.

What surprises, joys, frustrations did you feel or encounter then?

What advice would you give your younger self?

What support would you have wanted to receive during that time?

What did you want to know about your body?

What are you still wanting to know now concerning your body and sex?

What do you want for yourself now regarding sensual and sexual experiences?

Homework:

Do something sensual or sexual. Make love to yourself. Read erotica. Listen to music and dance
around. Paint in the nude. What is something sensual that would be healing for you? After you explore and experience, rest and notice what feelings
come up about feeling pleasure or enjoying your
sensual body. As you pay attention, you will clear
that programing that blocks your enjoyment and
creativity.

26 CLOSING THE CIRCLE

Welcome back into the spiral...

I have avoided writing to you because I am sad about the closing of our circle. I know the circle continues in the astral, but I will miss the exact sweetness of our little tribe. It will never be the same for me. It won't be better or worse; just different.

What will continue is the growth we have made and the friendships that have developed. My greatest wish is for you to have had at least one moment where you felt what support is. What love is. What connection and community feels like.

Maybe you have....maybe you haven't. Maybe you are clearer or more sure of your path after this process...maybe not. The truth is, this process has changed each of us. This circle has taken me to uncomfortable places and I have been transformed by the sisterhood. Wow...to the power of the Grand-

Mothers. They whisper and they shout. They hold us and they wait for us to start believing in ourselves.

No one can walk this life journey for us. But it sure is nice to have a little company on the path. Life is not for the faint of heart. Thank you for being willing to dive into this with me. You have all been teachers and fellow sisters. These lessons I take into my being and heart.

Prepare something to share for the closing ceremony weekend.

Get into a deep dialogue with the grandmothers, tone and mediate together. Ask them what you are meant to share with the group.

Things you can share:

A favorite food
A cup of tea
A story
A piece of art
A meditation
A part of your process

You will present this to the group. You can make a power point presentation, skip your turn, take us through a mediation. You know the drill; it's flowy and what you are comfortable with. I will speak with each of you individually before the weekend so that you can get some coaching or support from me for your "share".

As the circle closes the power lives on in you.

Sunday: Look at the archetype that you began with. What archetypes are you learning from. Which element do you feel you need in your life?

Share with the circle.

Calling in the animals for protection and communication.
Calling the grandmothers as our wise council.
Calling on the guardians of the light.
Calling the circle to a close.

Was there something so absurd that happened it made you laugh or cry? Who supported you this year. Where there any heroes - people who came through for you or experiences that went your way in a surprising manner? Give thanks for those moments.

Lunch

Sharing your gift with the circle.

This circle has served as a network or home base for your individual healing. This circle has not grown you; it has created a respite and a refugee from the harshness of life.

The strand we lifted up from the earth is laid back down. It is there for each of us to pull up and tap into when we need.

This circle exist in the astral forever and will always be available to you. Connecting to the astral is quite simple. Just sit in meditation and access it or lay down to a dream. Because you are embodied you need this support system. It has always been here. I have just reminded you of it.

Close the circle:

"Guardians and spirits of the North/South/East/ West, our circle is now complete. Farewell, spirits of the North, Grand Mothers and Old Ones of the Earth. We thank you for your presence. 'Til the next time Mighty Ones, go in peace but protect and guide each woman as she leaves this circle. We declare this scared circle closed."

Blow out the candles.

As the circle closes, the power lives on in you.

Made in the USA
Coppell, TX
31 August 2020

35341240R00104